Java™, XML, and JAXP

Java™, XML, and JAXP

Arthur Griffith

Wiley Computer Publishing

John Wiley & Sons, Inc.

NEW YORK · CHICHESTER · WEINHEIM · BRISBANE · SINGAPORE · TORONTO

Publisher: Robert Ipsen
Editor: Cary Sullivan
Developmental Editor: Scott Amerman
Associate Managing Editor: Penny Linskey
Associate New Media Editor: Brian Snapp
Text Design & Composition: Publishers' Design and Production Services, Inc.

Designations used by companies to distinguish their products are often claimed as trademarks. In all instances where John Wiley & Sons, Inc., is aware of a claim, the product names appear in initial capital or ALL CAPITAL LETTERS. Readers, however, should contact the appropriate companies for more complete information regarding trademarks and registration.

This book is printed on acid-free paper. ♾

Published by John Wiley & Sons, Inc.
Published simultaneously in Canada.

This publication is designed to provide accurate and authoritative information in regard to the subject matter covered. It is sold with the understanding that the publisher is not engaged in professional services. If professional advice or other expert assistance is required, the services of a competent professional person should be sought.

Library of Congress Cataloging-in-Publication Data:

ISBN: 0-471-20907-4

Printed in the United States of America.

10 9 8 7 6 5 4 3 2 1

Contents

Introduction

This book is intended to provide a solid foundation in XML to a Java programmer. It does this by describing XML and then using the API developed by Sun Microsystems to demonstrate simple examples of the fundamentals of XML document manipulation. You've heard of XML, and you have more than likely read something about it, but it all seems a bit mysterious. My hope is that, as you read this book, from time to time you say to yourself, "Oh. I see."

Every attempt was made to keep the focus of the book on its primary mission of explaining XML to a Java programmer. There are very few side issues mentioned.

There is an overwhelming amount of information about XML being made available in books, magazines, on the Internet, conferences, seminars, and even in mass mailings. It seems that everyone is either using XML or writing software so other people can use it. In the writing of this book, every attempt was made to distill the available information down to its essentials so the reader would be able to get a good basis from which to explore other areas of the subject. The intention of this book is that, after reading it, a person can proceed into any region of XML usage and technology and have a good understanding of the basics of what is taking place.

You will find that certain sections of the book are very tutorial-like, while other places are obviously intended for reference. In particular, Chapter 2 is almost completely reference information on the syntax for XML tags and the DTD used to add restrictions to the syntax. The rest of the reference material is found throughout the book in places where it is relevant.

One chapter discusses what could be considered a side issue. The chapter on Ant is about a utility that can be used to manage software development. But is not far off topic. Ant is an XML application that is written in Java and can be extended by your adding classes that process new instructions, that are defined as XML elements. And Sun provides Ant files with its JAXP distribution. It is the only large XML application discussed in the book.

Prerequisites

This is a beginner's book for XML, but it is not a beginner's book for general computing or programming. The following things are required of the reader:

1. The fundamentals of Java must be understood. This includes the concepts of inheritance, interfaces, static methods, properties, instantiation, and polymorphism. If you have sucessfully written a few classes in Java, and you have a good reference book, you have everything you need.

2. There should be some familiarity with the basic structure of HTML.

3. The reader must have Internet access and should have some rudimentary understanding of URLs and the process of transferring files from one location to another.

The following knowledge would be helpful but is not absolutely necessary:

1. Knowledge of the operation of lexical scanners and parsers.

2. An understanding of the basic structure of the ASCII and Unicode character sets.

How to Read This Book

To cover the entire subject, the book can be read straight through beginning with Chapter 1. And that is what I would suggest for someone entirely unfamiliar with XML and wanting to know about all of it. The examples are small and to the point—each one is designed to demonstrate just one idea—so it should take you quickly from one point to the next.

If you elect to read only portions of the book to extract information about certain aspects of XML, I would suggest that you at least skim through Chapters 1 and 2. These two chapters will provide you with a high-level overview of the Java software and a concise look at the structure of XML.

If you want a simple XML document reader, Chapters 3, 4, and 5 explain the SAX parser, which will read the document while checking its syntax and feed the document to your application in the form of a stream of tokens.

If you want a complete precedence-driven parser that gives you random access to the input document, Chapters 3, 6, and 7 describe the DOM parser.

If you are wanting to know how to process XML documents using XSL stylesheets, look at Chapter 8. Because XSL uses the same tree structure produced by the DOM parser, you will also need to be familiar with the information presented in Chapters 4 and 5.

If you are going to be starting a Java project you should look into Chapter 9 before you start. The Ant utility can be used to manage, cleanly and simply, a Java project of any size. I use it myself and have had great success with it.

Java™, XML, and JAXP

CHAPTER

1

Introduction to XML with JAXP

This chapter is an overview of some of the basic things you will need to know before you can understand the processing of XML documents using Java's Java API for XML Processing (JAXP). Although the Java application programming interface (API) is rather straightforward, you will need to understand how XML is constructed before you can clearly understand the sort of things that can be done with the API. The fundamental concepts described in this chapter include the fact that, like HTML, the XML language is derived from SGML. This kinship between XML and HTML has brought about the existence of a hybrid known as XHTML. There are two completely distinct parsers, named DOM and SAX, that can be used to read the contents of an XML document.

Java and XML

Java was designed to make it possible to write completely portable programs. XML was designed to make it possible to create completely portable data. In an ideal situation, using the two together will make for a completely portable software package that can communicate its data with any other completely portable software package. Nothing is absolutely perfect, but these two, used together, come about as close as anything that has been developed so far in terms of the ability to write a program that runs on any type of computer and can swap data with any other type of computer.

The JAXP package is a set of Java classes that implements XML document parsers, supplies methods that can be used to manipulate the parsed data, and has special transformation processors to automate the conversion of data from XML to another form. For example, the other form can be a database record layout ready for storage, an HTML Web page ready for display, or simply a textual layout ready for printing.

One of the outstanding features of XML is its fundamental simplicity. Once you understand how tags are used to create elements, it is easy to manually read and write XML documents. With this basic XML understanding, and with knowledge of the Java language, it is a straightforward process to understand the relationship between XML and the Java API for manipulating XML. There are only a few classes in this API, and it is only a matter of creating the appropriate set of objects, and they will supply the methods you can call to manipulate the contents of an XML document. With these basic concepts understood, and with the simplicity of the constructs involved, you can design and write programs while concentrating mostly on the problem you are trying to solve, not on the mechanics of getting it done.

Java, the Language

Following are some characteristics of Java that make it ideal for use as a language to manipulate XML documents:

- **The JAXP is now a part of standard Java.** It contains all of the classes and interfaces that you need for parsing and processing an XML document. It also contains methods that can be used to automate the transformation process of converting an XML document into an entirely different form.

- **The fundamental Java stream IO can be used for input of XML documents and output of the results of processing.** This means that your application is able to process files stored remotely on the Internet just as easily as the ones on the local disk. Once a stream has been established to a file, the rest of the application can use streaming input and output without having to know anything about the location at the other end of the stream. You can write your application just once and know that it will work no matter how the data needs to be fed to or extracted from it.

- **The majority of installed Web servers are capable of running Java applications to dynamically generate Web pages**. This means that, using the JAXP, the set of Java classes that provide the methods to be used to manage XML documents, it becomes a very simple matter to transform data from an XML format to HTML format as a response to a request made from a remote Web browser. All of the software you need, from receiving the request through formatting the data to transmitting the response, is ready and waiting. About all that is left to do is decide how you want the Web page to appear and then write the Java code to lay it out.

- **Portability applies to anything written in Java**. Using Java and its built-in JAXP allows you to run the application on any computer that has a Java Virtual Machine installed. And, because XML is also portable, the result is an almost universally portable system and can be used in exactly the same way on any computer.

To fully understand the concepts discussed in the following paragraphs and chapters, you should be familiar with Java, or familiarize yourself with the Java programming language using Java tutorials. To understand how these classes do their jobs, you will only need to understand Java classes, objects, interfaces, and methods. There is nothing more complicated than a static method returning an object that implements an interface; if you understand these fundamentals, you will have no problem with anything in this book.

XML, the Language

XML stands for Extensible Markup Language. These three words are actually a very accurate description. It is a nonprocedural programming *language*, which means that things written in the language are not so much commands as they are descriptions of a condition or state. Like almost all programming languages, XML is written as human-readable text, in such a form that humans as well as programs can read and understand the instructions.

The XML language is used to *mark up* a document so that the reader (usually a program) can identify each piece of the document and determine its characteristics by examining the tags it contains. A tag can be named anything you would like, but it only has meaning if the program reading the document already knows the tag name. XML is also *extensible* because you can invent as many markup tags as you need as you go along; all you need to do is make sure the reader of the document knows the meanings of your tags. In fact, there are no markup tags defined as part of XML. The creator of an XML document invents whatever tags are necessary for a full description of the document being marked up.

There is a common misconception that the purpose of XML is to format and display data. That is not what it is for. Its purpose is to store data in a form that can be easily read and analyzed. It is quite common to use XML to store data and use the descriptive XML tags to specify how it should be displayed, but this not an inherent part of XML. It is also very common to write applications that convert XML data into HTML for display. And, because XML and HTML are so similar in their basic syntax, it is possible to use the tag names defined for HTML in an XML document and then use a Web browser to display it as if it were HTML. A special name for this type of XML document is XHTML, but it is just a special case of XML.

A file, or other entity, containing XML-formatted data is referred to as a *document*. This term carries a broad interpretation because XML is used to format many different kinds of information, some of which is never intended for human use (such as data being transferred from one database to another). The following examples show how tags can be used to mark up documents. An XML document can be for any purpose and can take any form it needs to fit that purpose, but generally speaking, there are two categories of XML documents. An XML document can be storage for text that is intended to be formatted and presented in a readable format. Or it can be a convenient form for packaging data records for transmission from one place to another, or simply for storage, in a portable format. The following is an example of text that can be formatted for display:

```
<paragraph>
The purpose of this type of XML document is to use
<italic>tags</italic> in such a way that the software that
reads the document will be able to <underline>organize</underline>
and <underline>format</underline> the text in such a way that
it is more presentable and easier to read.
</paragraph>
```

This form of XML looks a lot like HTML. In fact, this form of XML and HTML both serve exactly the same purpose: to allow the software reading the document to extract things from it and also to use the tags as formatting instructions to create a display from the extracted text.

The same basic form can be used to package data, as in the following example:

```
<person>
   <name>Karan Dirsham</name>
   <street>8080 Holly Lane</street>
   <city>Anchor Point</city>
   <state>Alaska</state>
   <zip>99603</zip>
</person>
```

This second form is more like a collection of fields that go to make up a data record, and used this way, it can be a very convenient method for storing data and transmitting information among otherwise incompatible systems. All that is necessary for successful data reception of transmitted data is for the recipient to understand the meanings of the tags and be able to extract the data from them. Of course, by using the appropriate application to read and process the data, any XML document can be easily formatted for display. The process of extraction and formatting XML data is the primary subject of this book.

Attributes can be used to specify options that further refine the meaning of the tags to the process reading the document. These attributes can be used both for data definition and for formatting. For example, the following code has attributes:

```
<person font="Courier">
   <name type="first" enhance="bold">Janie</name>
   <name type="last" enhance="underline">Rorick</name>
</person>
```

Any program reading this document can apply its own interpretation to the meanings of the tags and the options. No formatting information is included in an XML document. All formatting is left entirely to the process reading and interpreting the XML document. One program could read a document containing this example and take the bold option to mean a different font, another could take it to mean a larger font, and another could use it as an instruction to underline the text or display it in a different color. Or the bold option could be ignored altogether. The only thing XML knows about the attribute is the syntax required to include it with a tag.

If you have worked with HTML, you can see the similarities in the syntax of HTML and XML. They are similar enough that it is possible to write an XML document and use only tag names known to a particular Web browser and then have that Web browser read the document and impose its interpretations on the tags and options and result in a displayed page. A displayable XML document is written often enough that a document of this type has a special name; it is called XHTML. There is more information about XHTML later in this chapter.

XML is a *nonprocedural* computer language, as opposed to a *procedural* language such as Java. A procedural language is one that consists of lists of instruction that are expected to be obeyed one by one, usually in order from top to bottom. A nonprocedural language is one that expects all of its instructions to be executed as if they were all being executed simultaneously and, if necessary, to react to one another to create an overall state or set of states. An example of nonprocedural processing is a spreadsheet in which all the cells in the sheet that contain equations have their values calculated at once, creating a static state of constant values displayed in the cells. This same sort of thing happens in a Web browser where the HTML tags define the state (layout, colors, text, pictures, fonts, and so on) that determines the appearance of a Web page.

DTD

DTD stands for Document Type Definition. Although DTD is normally treated separately from XML tags, has a different syntax, and serves a different purpose, it is very much a part of the XML language. The DTD section of an XML document is used to define the names and syntax of the elements that can be used in the document. There are several steps involved in the creation and application of a DTD definition, and Chapter 2 contains explanations of those steps along with a number of examples. Its source can be included inline inside an XML document, or it can be stored in a separate document from the XML text and tags. Because its purpose is to specify the correct format of a marked up document, DTD is most useful if it is made available to several documents and is most often stored in a file separate from any XML document, which enables it to be accessed from any number of XML documents. For the sake of simplicity, however, most of the examples in this book have a simple DTD included as part of the XML document.

DTD enables you to further refine the syntactical requirements of a set of XML markup rules. In a DTD you can specify the allowed and disallowed content of each tag that is to appear in an XML document. That takes at least a third of Chapter 2. DTD has its limitations, but there are many different things that can be done by using it. You can specify which elements are allowed to appear inside other elements as well as which elements are required and where they are required. You can specify which attributes are valid for each tag and even specify the set of possible values for each one. You can create macro-like objects (called *entities*) that are expanded into text as the XML document is parsed. All of this is explored in Chapter 2.

An XML document that conforms to the fundamental syntax of markup tags is called *well-formed*. To be a well-formed document, all elements must have matching opening and closing tags, and the tags must be nested properly. For example, the expression `<p><b>text</b></p>` is well-formed because the opening tags, `<p><b>`, have closing tags, `</b></p>`, and they are nested properly. To be well-formed every closing tag must be a match with the most recent tag that is still open. In short, all tags must be closed in the exact reverse order in which they were opened. The expressions `<p><b>text</b>` and `<p><b>text</p></b>` are not well-formed.

An XML document that conforms to the rules of its DTD is referred to as a *valid* document. For a document to be successfully tested as being valid, it must also be well-formed. Some parsers can check the document against the DTD definitions and throw an exception if the document is not valid.

Use of DTDs is very important to the portability of XML. If a DTD is well written (that is, if all the tags are defined properly), a process can be written that will be able to read and interpret any XML data from any document that conforms to the rules of the DTD.

A single XML document can use more than one DTD. However, this multiple DTD use can result in a naming collision. If two or more DTDs define a tag by the same name, they will more than likely define that tag as having different characteristics. For example, one could be defined as requiring a font attribute, whereas the other has no such attribute. This problem is solved by using device known as a *namespace*. An element specified as being from one namespace is distinct from one of the same name from another namespace. For example, if a pair of DTDs both include a definition for an element with the tag name `selectable`, one DTD could be declared in the namespace `max` and the other in the namespace `scrim`; then there would be the two distinct tag names `max:selectable` and `scrim:selectable` available for use in the document. Examples using namespaces are explained in Chapter 2.

XSL

XSL stands for XML Stylesheet Language. It is used as a set of instructions for the translation of the content of an XML document into another form—usually a presentation form intended to be displayed to a human. An XSL program is actually, in itself, a document that adheres to the syntax of XML. It contains a set of detailed instructions for extracting data from another XML document and converting it to a new format. Performing such transformation is the subject of Chapter 8.

The process of using XSL to change the format of the data is known as *transformation*. Transformation methods are built into the JAXP that can be used to perform any data format translation you define in an XSL document. These transformations can be programmed directly into Java instead of using XSL, but XSL simplifies things by taking care of some of the underlying mechanics, such as walking through the memory-resident parse tree to examine the source document. It also supplies you with some built-in methods for doing commonly performed tasks such as configuring the parser and handling error conditions.

XSL performs a function—supplying human-readable data—that is every bit as important as XML itself. With the single exception of robotics, all the software in the world is ultimately used to display data to humans. Nothing is ever stored in a database without the expectation that it will be extracted and presented in some human-readable format. In fact, presenting readable data is the entire purpose of the Internet. Operating systems and computer language compilers only exist to support and create other programs that, in turn, directly or indirectly present data in a form that can be understood by humans.

SAX

SAX stands for Simple API for XML. It is a collection of Java methods that can be used to read an XML document and parse it in such a way that each of the individual pieces of the input are supplied to your program. It is a very rudimentary form of parsing that is not much more than a lexical scan: It reads the input, determines the type of things it encounters (it recognizes the format of the nested tags and separates out the text that is the data portion of the document), and supplies them to your program in the same order in which they appear in the document.

The form of the data coming from a SAX parser can be very useful for streaming operations such as a direct translation of tags or text into another form, with no changes in order. If your application needs to switch things around, however, it will be necessary for it to keep copies of the data so it can be reorganized. In many cases, it would be easier to parse using the DOM parser. The SAX parser has the advantage of being fast and small because it doesn't hold anything in memory once it has moved on to the next input item in the input document.

There are two versions of SAX. The original version is SAX 1.0 (also called SAX1). The current version is SAX 2.0 (also called SAX2). SAX2 is an extension of the definitions of SAX 1.0 to include things such as the ability to specify names using namespaces. Both SAX1 and SAX2 are a part of JAXP. Because SAX1 is still a part of JAXP, programs based on it will work , but much of it has been deprecated in the API to promote use of SAX2 in all newly written programs. Only SAX2 is discussed in the following chapters because it does everything SAX1 does and more.

DOM

DOM stands for Document Object Model. It is a collection of Java methods that enable your program to parse an input document into a memory-resident tree of nodes that maintains the relationships found in the original input document. There are also methods that enable your application to walk freely about the tree and extract the information stored there.

The internal form of the data tree resulting from a DOM parse is quite convenient if you are going to be accessing document content out of order. That is, if your program needs to rearrange the incoming data for its output, or if it needs to move around the document and select data in random-access order, you should find that the DOM document tree will provide what you need for doing this. You can search for things in the tree and pull out what you need without regard to where it appeared in the input document. One disadvantage of DOM is that a large document will take up a lot of space because the entire document is held in memory. With modern operating systems, however, the document would need to be extremely large before it would adversely affect anything. DOM also has the disadvantage of being more complicated to use than SAX. Because DOM can randomly access the stored data, the API for it is necessarily more complex. Although DOM is more complicated to use than SAX, it can be used to do much more. For more details about how DOM works, see Chapters 3, 6, and 7.

Internally in the JAXP, the DOM parser actually uses SAX as its lexical scanner. That is, a SAX parser is used to read the document and break it down into a stream of its components, and the DOM software takes this token stream and constructs a tree from it. This is why it is best to have an understanding of SAX before trying to get a clear idea of how JAXP DOM works. Although you may never use SAX directly, it's a good idea to know how it works and how the incoming document is broken down. At the very least, you will need to be familiar with the meaning of its error messages and how to process them in your application, which means you will need to know how SAX works. For more details, see Chapters 3, 4, and 5

SGML

SGML stands for Standard Generalized Markup Language. This is the parent markup language of XML and HTML, which were both derived as special-purpose subsets of SGML. Included in the 500-page SGML specification document is a definition of the system for organizing and tagging elements in a document. It became a standard with the International Organization of Standards (ISO) in 1986, but the specification had actually been in use some time before that. It was designed to manage large documents so that they could be frequently changed and also printed. It is a large language definition and too difficult to actually implement, which has resulted in the subsets XML and HTML.

XML works well being a subset of SGML because the complexity of SGML isn't necessary to do all of the tagging and transforming that needs to be done. Being a practical subset makes it much easier to write a parser for XML. Because of the reduction in complexity of the language, XML documents are smaller and easier to create than SGML documents would be. For example, where SGML always requires the presence of a DTD, in XML the DTD is largely optional. If you are going to validate the correctness of an XML document, the DTD is necessary, but otherwise it can be omitted.

XML is a bit closer to being like SGML than is HTML. For one thing, HTML is filled with ambiguities because it allows things like an opening tag that has no closing tag to match it. This prevents any attempts to standardize HTML because a parser cannot predict what it will find. And many HTML extensions and modifications apply in one place but do not apply in another. Although XML is extensible—you can add all the tag types you wish—it is very strict in the way it allows you to do it. Like SGML, the formatting of XML can be controlled by XSL documents used for transformations.

XHTML

XHTML stands for Extensible Hypertext Markup Language. An XHTML document is a hybrid of XML and HTML in such a way that it is syntactically correct for both of them. That is, although an XHTML document can be displayed by a Web browser, it can also be parsed into its component parts by a SAX or DOM parser. Both XML and HTML are subsets of SGML, so the only problem in combining the two into XHTML was in dealing with the places where HTML had departed from the standard format. Most obvious are the many opening tags in HTML that do not have closing tags to match them and the fact that tag nesting is not required.

XHTML was conceived so that, once Web browsers were capable of dealing with the strict and standard forms required for XML, a more standardized form of Web page could evolve. With XML it is relatively easy to introduce new forms by defining additional elements and attributes, and because this same technique is part of XHTML, it will allow the smooth integration of new features with the existing ones. This capability is particularly attractive because alternate ways of accessing the Internet are constantly being developed. The presence of a standard, parsable Web page will allow easier modification to the display format for new demands, such as the special requirements of hand-held computers.

There is a fundamental difference between XML and HTML. XML *is* an SGML, while HTML is an *application* of SGML. That is, SGML does not have any tag names defined and neither does XML. For both XML and SGML, a DTD must be used to define and provide meanings for element names. On the other hand, HTML has a set of element names already defined. The element names of HTML are the ones that have a meaning to the Web browser attempting to format the page. This fundamental difference between XML and HTML can be overcome by the creation of a DTD that defines the syntax for all the elements that are used in HTML. With such a DTD in place, an XML document that adheres to the DTD's definitions will also be an HTML document, and thus it can be displayed using a Web browser.

JAXP

JAXP stands for Java API for XML Processing. It is a set of Java classes and interfaces specifically designed to be used in a program to make it capable of reading, manipulating, and writing XML-formatted data.

It includes complete parsers for SAX1 and SAX2 and the two types of DOM: DOM Level 1 and DOM Level 2. Most of this book explores the use of parsers in extracting data from an XML document. More information on both of these parsers is the subject of Chapter 3. There are examples of using the SAX parsers in Chapters 4 and 5 and of the DOM parsers in Chapters 6 and 7. All of the parsers check whether a document is well-formed, and the parsers can be used in validating or nonvalidating mode, as described in the DTD section earlier in this chapter. There is also an extensive API that can be used to access the data resulting from any of these parsers. And although SAX1 and DOM Level 1 are both present and working, the API for them is deprecated. Anything you need to do can be accomplished with just the SAX2 and DOM Level 2 API.

The simplest way to get a copy of JAXP is to download and install the latest copy of Java from Sun at http://java.sun.com. Beginning with Java version 1.4, the JAXP API is included as part of Java 2 Standard Edition. It is also a part of the Java 1.3 Enterprise Edition. If you want to use JAXP with a prior version of Java, you can get a copy of it from the Web site http://java.sun.com/xml. You can use JAXP version 1.1 with the Java Software Development Kit (SDK) version 1.1.8 or newer.

If, for some reason, you are staying with an older version of Java and downloading JAXP as a separate API, you will need to download the documentation separately. This documentation is in the form of a set of HTML pages generated from the source code by the standard javadoc utility. It is in the same format as the documentation for the rest of Java. There are two ways to install the standalone JAXP: You can include its jar files in the same directories as your Java installation, or you can install them in their own directories. If you do not elect to include them with Java, you will need to specify the `classpath` settings when either compiling or running a JAXP application.

Ant

Ant is a tool used to compile Java classes. It isn't limited to Java; it can be used for your entire software development project. It performs the same job as the traditional make utility by compiling only the programs that need to be compiled, but it has some special features that cause it to work very will with Java. For one thing, it understands the Java package organization and can use it when checking dependencies. It is an XML application and, as such, uses an XML file as its input control file (much like the make utility uses a `makefile`) to determine which modules to compile. The Java classes of Ant are available in source code form, so you can, by extending the existing classes, add any new commands and processing that you would like.

When compiling Java, Ant compares the timestamp of the source files to timestamp of the class files to determine which Java source files need to be compiled. Also, Ant knows about the relationship between Java directory trees and packages, so it is capable of descending your source tree properly to create classes within several packages.

For more information about Ant, with examples, see Chapter 9. The Web site for Ant is http://jakarta.apache.org/ant/.

Summary

This chapter is an overview of the basics. You should now have some idea of what JAXP is designed to do and a rough idea of how it does it. Using JAXP, a Java program is capable of reading an XML document and analyzing its various parts for meaning or formatting. There is more than one way to read a document: You can do it in a sequential manner with a SAX parser or browse about the document randomly by using a DOM parser.

The next chapter takes a detailed look at the syntax of an XML document. As you will see, its tags and content are straightforward and easy to read and write. The complexities of the syntax are all contained in the DTD portion. Chapter 2 describes the syntax and is designed to make it easy for you to use as a reference later.

XML Document Format

This chapter examines the syntactical format of an XML document. At the top of each document is a heading making the declaration that it is an XML document. Next there is an optional Document Type Definition (DTD) that defines some specific syntax rules that must be followed for the remainder of the document. Finally, the body of the document itself consists of text and the tags that are used to mark it up.

The body of an XML document contains text marked with tags that describe the text. The original intent of XML was to ensure that humans could easily read and write XML documents, so all XML documents contain only text. When binary data—such as an image or an audio file—must be included, the binary file is stored separately, and the XML document contains a reference to that file.

All of the text of an XML document is included between pairs of tags. If you are familiar with HTML, you know how this works (although XML is much more strict about it than HTML). A tag can be identified by its name, and every opening tag has a closing tag with the text itself sandwiched between them. Unlike HTML, when writing an XML document, you can create your own tag names. In creating your own tag names, however, it is essential that you use tags known to the process that will receive and read the XML document. The program must recognize what the tags are and what they mean. Most of this book concerns itself with processes that read XML documents and process tag data.

Very much a child of the Internet, XML makes it easy to complete the text of a document by including links to data and text files stored in remote locations. In fact, the

XML language itself has the ability to require the presence of data resources in a remote location. These resources can be simply data, or they can be schema information used to validate the correctness of the tags and the general format of a document. This means that the *parser*—the program that reads an XML document—must be able to read information from another host on the Internet.

There are really two syntaxes built into XML. One is the tag-based form used for laying out the document itself, and the other is the DTD syntax that can be used by the parser to validate the form and content of the text and attributes of tags throughout the document. In other words, the tags define the content of a document, and the DTD can be used by the parser as a sort of XML watchdog by making sure that the tags are used correctly. As you will see in this chapter, the syntax is quite different and the two are in separate locations in the document. The DTD is optional in that it carries no data; the exact same XML document can be written with or without the DTD.

Some General Notes about Syntax

The syntax of XML allows you to create a document in any format you would like, and at the same time, it allows you to use tagging to restrict or define the content any way you would like. To achieve this, the body of an XML document is free-form text intermixed with tags that specify the context of the text. These tags are known as *markup* and are designed to be read and processed by an XML parser. The tags have a distinct format that distinguishes them from the textual content of the document.

Names

Tag names are made up from specific characters. The first character of a name must be one of the following:

```
A-Z  a-z  _  :
```

Following the first character of the name, the rest of the characters must each be one of the following:

```
A-Z  a-z  .  -  _  :
```

Upper- and lowercase characters are distinct. These are all characters from the ASCII character set. If you are using Unicode, you can also use the alphabetic characters from any other language as name starters and as internal name characters. As you can see, digits are not allowed in a name, and a name cannot begin with a period or a hyphen (minus sign). A name can be of any length.

There is a concept in XML that deals with grouping names into *namespaces* to simplify the organization of complicated documents. There are more details on this later in the chapter. If a name contains a colon, it can actually be two names; the part before the colon is the namespace in which the name is found, and the part after the colon is the actual name. Because the specification of namespace came along after the specification for XML, and is still in a separate document, the use of colons is valid in any name. However, namespace uses this fact to add some scoping to names.

Names beginning with the three-letter sequence XML (upper- or lowercase in any combination) are all reserved for future use. You may be able to use a name starting with these three letters and find that it is not currently reserved, but it may become reserved in some future version of XML.

Strings

Throughout XML you will find quoted strings. The examples in this book almost exclusively use double quotes to create these strings, but it doesn't have to be that way. It's just a matter of style and personal preference. Anywhere you see a pair of double quotes defining a string, a pair of single quotes (apostrophes) could have been used. That is:

```
"This is a string"
```

is exactly the same as:

```
'This is a string'
```

The ability to select the type of quotes makes it convenient for including either single or double quotes as a character inside a string. For example, if you need to include a single quote character inside a string, simply create the string using double quotes, like this:

```
"This won't cause a problem"
```

The same is true for the opposite situation; you can include double quotes in a string created using single quotes. For another way to insert quotes, and other special characters, see the discussion on entities later in this chapter.

Whitespace

The whitespace characters are listed Table 2.1. All other valid characters, including ones like backspace and form feed, are assumed to be part of the XML document.

The handling of whitespace is largely up to the application program reading the document, but there are some actions that will be taken automatically by the parser unless

Table 2.1   The Whitespace Characters

NAME	HEXADECIMAL VALUE
space	0x20
tab	0x09
line feed	0x0A
carriage return	0x0D

you specify otherwise. For example, it's normal for the parser to strip out some of the whitespace characters to allow the document to be formatted in a readable fashion. If you've worked with HTML, you're familiar with this type of action. For example, it's customary to indent the tags to help indicate which ones are nested inside others, as follows:

```
<outer>
    <inner>
        <bold>Text of the inner tag.</bold>
    </inner>
<outer>
```

In this example it is perfectly all right for the parser to strip out all of the whitespace between the tags. However, if you have text that should retain all of its whitespace characters exactly as written, you can command the parser to not make any changes by using the xml:space attribute as follows:

```
<poem xml:space="preserve">
    Algy met a bear.
    The bear was bulgy.
    The bulge was Algy.
</poem>
```

If the spacing is allowed to default, however, there is no standard way that whitespace is to be handled by the parser, and your application would have no way of knowing how the text was originally formatted. An example is:

```
<outer>
    <inner>
        Text of the inner tag.
    </inner>
<outer>
```

This example demonstrates a situation where the newline character at the end of the text and the blanks in front of it could each be reduced to a single space (as is done in HTML). The problem is that different parsers may handle this type of situation in different ways; some will leave them in and others will strip them out.

Bottom line: Use xml:space="preserve" in every case where whitespace retention is important. Otherwise, assume that any sequence of two or more whitespace characters will be reduced to a single space. But remember that the default action will vary from one parser to the next; there are even parsers that ignore any settings you may have for xml:space.

A Fundamental XML Document

A simple XML document is quite readable by a human because it is written in plain text as opposed to binary code. If you're familiar with HTML, you'll have no problem recognizing the form of the following simple document. The data contained in the document shown in Listing 2.1, which is the text outside of the tags, lists the names and contact information of a couple of people.

The first line of Listing 2.1 identifies it as an XML document. This is not strictly required, but it is a very good idea to include it at the top of every document so the type and version of your document can be verified. This type of instruction is known as a *processing instruction* (PI) because its purpose is to pass instructions to the process that will be reading the document.

The data contained in the document is the text, and each piece of text is enclosed between a pair of tags—one opening and one closing tag—and the tags specify the meaning of the text. For example, the name of each person is preceded by a <name> tag and is terminated by a </name> tag. These tags give the data in an XML document identity

Notice how the tag pairs are nested one inside the other. The outermost tag pair, which is <folks> at the top and </folks> at the bottom, is called the *root tag*. The outermost pair of tags in every XML document are the root tags. All of the text of an XML document is enclosed by the root tag pair, and, inside the pair of root tags, there are normally other tag pairs that define pieces of the text further.

XML Declaration

Every XML document should have, as its first line, an XML declaration that specifies the version number. The current, and only, version of XML is 1.0, so a minimum declaration line looks like the following:

```
<?xml version="1.0"?>
```

This declaration is not an actual XML requirement, but it's a very good idea. It's important to include the version number because it's possible that there will be future versions of XML that contain features not compatible with version 1.0, and the version number may be crucial to how future parsers deal with XML documents.

```
<?xml version="1.0"?>
<folks>
    <person>
        <name>Bertha D. Blues</name>
        <phone>907 555-8901</phone>
        <email>bertha@xyz.net</email>
    </person>
    <person>
        <name>Fred Drew</name>
        <phone>907 555-9921</phone>
        <email>fred@xyz.net</email>
    </person>
</folks>
```

Listing 2.1 A Simple XML Document

Other information is often included with the declaration. The following example specifies that the text is Unicode in a compressed form (in other words, it's an ASCII file that allows for expanded 16-bit Unicode characters). Also, this declaration specifies that the XML document doesn't make references to external documents, so it can be read and used as completely self-contained data.

```
<?xml version="1.0" encoding="UTF-8" standalone="yes"?>
```

The `encoding` value is the name of the character set used to write the XML document. For the `encoding` value to have any meaning, the name must be recognized by the program reading and processing the document. Because Java, by default, inputs text as `UTF-8`, there's no need to specify the encoding unless you're going to do something unusual. If you know the document will be limited to 7-bit ASCII, you can declare the encoding to be `"US-ASCII"`. Also, a declaration of `"UTF-8"` works for standard 7-bit ASCII because `UTF-8` includes all of the ASCII characters (values from 0x00 through 0x7F), but it'll also allow for the recognition of properly encoded Unicode characters. Java easily reads and writes this format without you having to specify anything else. If the text uses what is commonly called the extended ASCII characters (values from 0x10 through 0xFF), the encoding should be one of the names `"ISO-8859-1"` through `"ISO-8859-9"` and cannot be `"US-ASCII"` or `"UTF-8"`.

There are many other encodings possible. If you're going to need some special encoding, it would be best to use one of the Internet Assigned Numbers Authority (IANA) character-set names. For the official and exhaustive list take a look at http://www.iana.org/assignments/character-sets.

The `standalone` attribute specifies whether external documents are referenced from inside this XML document. If `standalone` is `"yes"`, it specifies that there are no external documents referenced, and the parser, knowing it only needs to work with this one file, can execute in a way that makes the processing more efficient. If it is `"no"`, the document may—but doesn't necessarily have to—refer to an external document.

The declaration is in the form of a PI that begins with the character pair `<?` and is terminated by `?>`. This XML declaration is a very special PI that appears at the top of every document. There's more information on the purpose and form of PIs later in this chapter.

XML Tags and Elements

An XML tag begins with a less-than character, ends with a greater-than character, and contains an identifying name. Each XML tag has an identifying name that begins with a letter or an underscore character and can contain letters, digits, periods, hyphens, and underscores. You can also include a colon as part of the name, but that is used for specifying namespaces, which are described later in this chapter.

There are some reserved names that you can't use for any other purpose. Any name that begins with `xml` (or `XML`, or any other upper- and lowercase combination) should not be used. Names that begin with these three letters are reserved for system use. An example of this is the name `xmlns` used for namespaces. There is a more complete definition of name formats earlier in this chapter.

All tags have both an opening and a closing. In the following example the opening tag is `<paragraph>` and the closing tag is `</paragraph>`. The opening and closing tags have the same name. An opening tag has no slash character, whereas the closing tag always has one:

```
<paragraph>The running board fell off!</paragraph>
```

A tag pair, along with any text or other tag pairs it contains, is a single unit known as an *element*. An element may contain any amount of text and any number of elements. An XML document is made up of a collection of elements nested one inside the other. The outermost element is the *root element*.

NOTE XML names are case sensitive. The tags <subtitle>, <Subtitle>, <SubTitle>, and <SUBTITLE> are all different tags. Likewise, keywords of the XML language are case sensitive; although DOCTYPE and ELEMENT are both keywords in XML, Doctype and element are not.

An element isn't required to contain anything between its opening and closing tags. The following is an example of an empty element:

```
<paragraph></paragraph>
```

Empty elements occur often enough that there's a special shorthand notation for them. Following is an example of the shorthand notation for an empty element:

```
<paragraph/>
```

In this example, there's only one tag, but because the trailing slash is included, it acts as both the opening and closing tag of an empty element.

Attributes

It's possible to specify one or more attributes as part of an opening tag. The attributes normally modify or amplify the meaning of the tag. For example, the following form could be used to specify the font to be applied to the text of a paragraph:

```
<paragraph font="Times">The running board fell off!</paragraph>
```

All attributes take this same form. There is an attribute name (`font` in this example), followed by an equal sign and a quoted string. The quoted string is the value of the named attribute. It is possible to include more than one attribute with a tag. An example is:

```
<section type="sidebar" font="Courier" style="bold">Text</section>
```

As with all quoted strings in XML, you can use double quotes or single quotes to specify the value. An example is:

```
<paragraph font='Times'>The running board fell off!</paragraph>
```

The ability to use more than one kind of quote is more than a simple convenience. It provides an easy way to include quote marks inside the attribute value, such as:

```
<division title="Don't quit"></title>
```

Single and double quote characters, along with other special characters, can also be inserted by using the predefined entities describe in the "Entities" section of this chapter.
Attributes can be specified inside the short form of empty elements, like this:

```
<division title="Don't quit"/>
```

Comments

Anywhere you can put a tag, you can put a comment. A comment is normally ignored by the process reading the document; it is only used to clarify the following or surround XML document. A comment begins with the four-character sequence < ! - - and ends with the three-character sequence - - >, such as:

```
<!-- This is the form of a simple comment -->
```

Because XML is a free-form language, a single comment can spread across several lines and look like the following:

```
<!--
    This is a comment that continues for more than
    one line. This form can be used for a descriptive block
    of text at the top or to try to make sense of some
    some XML element that could be somewhat obscure.
-->
```

NOTE There's one limitation to the contents of a comment. The two-character sequence - - cannot be included in the body of a comment. This limitation exists to accommodate very rudimentary parsers.

The Character Entities

An entity is a special name that you include in your XML text in such a way that it's replaced with something else by the parser. For example, because the left angle bracket character is used to define the start of a tag, you need to do something special to insert it into your text. This is accomplished by using the predefined entity name lt. To use an entity, precede it with an ampersand and terminate it with a semicolon. An example is:

```
<relation>Which proves that x &lt; a + b.</relation>
```

Table 2.2   The XML Predefined Entities

ENTITY	PRODUCES	DESCRIPTION
&	&	Ampersand
'	'	Single quote (apostrophe)
>	>	Greater than
<	<	Less than
"	"	Double quote

Once this element is parsed, the resulting string will look like the following:

```
Which proves that x < a + b.
```

Table 2.2 lists the predefined entities that enable you to insert characters that would otherwise cause problems with the parser.

You can use an entity to insert any character by specifying the Unicode or ASCII numeric value of the character. This comes in handy when you want to insert a character that has no key on your keyboard, such as a Greek character. This is particularly true of Unicode because it includes the characters from every alphabet. The example in Listing 2.2 demonstrates the two different ways of specifying a Greek alphabet character:

Just like any other entity, when specifying a numeric value, you have to precede the entity with an ampersand and terminate it with a semicolon. The # character is used to indicate a numeric entity. If the first character in the number is a small x, the digits are interpreted as hexadecimal digits; otherwise, they are assumed to be decimal digits. You can define entities of your own by including their definitions in the DTD, as described later in this chapter.

```
<?xml version="1.0"?>

<charents>
    <fromhex>
        The character &#x03A3; is an uppercase sigma.
    </fromhex>
    <fromdec>
        The character &#931; is an uppercase sigma.
    </fromdec>
</charents>
```

Listing 2.2   An XML Document Containing Special Characters

```
<?xml version="1.0"?>

<progs>>
    <function>
    <![CDATA[
        int frammis() {
            if((a > b) && (a < 3.4))
                return(1);
            return(0);
        }
    ]]>
    </function>
</progs>
```

Listing 2.3   Using a CDATA Section for Special Formatting

The CDATA Section

If your text contains a lot of characters that could cause an XML parser problems, you can get the parser to accept these characters directly without having to string together a lot of the predefined entities. You can place the offending text inside a CDATA section and the special characters will be ignored. The example in Listing 2.3 shows how to include some source code without worrying about the individual characters:

The CDATA section begins with the nine-character string <![CDATA[and ends with the three-character sequence]]>. The text must both be written exactly as you want it to be formatted; no unwanted whitespaces can be inserted inside a CDATA section. The text between the opening and closing of the section is completely ignored by the parser. This means that the only character or sequence of characters that can't be included inside a CDATA section is the three-character string]]>.

NOTE There is also a CDATA in DTD that should not be confused with this one. They are for entirely different purposes and are not related.

DTD

The tags in an XML file are, by default, completely free form as long as the basic syntax of the XML language is followed. You can, however, impose syntactic specifications on each of the tag names by including a DTD in your XML document. Remember, a DTD doesn't add any meaning to the elements of a document; it only refines and extends the syntactic requirements. You can use the DTD to specify the type of data that can be included in an element, the relative order and position of the elements, and which elements can be nested inside other elements.

The DTD syntax is quite different from that of the rest of the XML document. It primarily consists of a list of all the tag names and a specification of the form each one will take.

You can include the text of the DTD as part of the XML document itself, or you can put the DTD into a separate file and simply refer to the file from the XML document. The advantage of having the DTD as a separate file is that you can use it to define the tag format for any number of XML documents. In fact, you can combine formats together by having a single XML document use the formatting defined in more than one DTD file. The disadvantage of having the DTD as a separate file is that if you send the XML document to someone else, they will normally need to use the same DTD file so that the syntax of both the form and content of the elements can be recognized.

NOTE Even though the syntax of DTD is decidedly different from the rest of XML, and the presence of DTD is optional, it's still a part of the XML language. The DTD text is read and processed by the same parser that reads and processes the other parts of an XML document.

Single File

The document in Listing 2.4 shows how to use the DOCTYPE keyword to insert the text of the DTD information inside the XML document.

Notice that standalone is set to "yes" in Listing 2.4 to indicate that everything is contained in a single file. It would have been perfectly valid to set standalone to "no" so that the parser would be ready to handle multiple files even though only one file is used. Some parsers, however, will be more efficient if they know up front that everything is going to be in one file.

To specify the DTD information, the keyword DOCTYPE is used as shown in Listing 2.4. Everything inside the opening bracket and closing bracket of the DOCTYPE declaration is a part of the DTD. The DOCTYPE declaration itself requires the name of the root element (in this example it's the folks element) of the XML document.

In this example DTD there are five ELEMENT declarations. An ELEMENT declaration specifies the contents of an element. The root element, named folks, is allowed to contain only person elements. The number of person elements that can be contained is specified by the asterisk modifier, which means there may be zero or more person elements listed inside a folks element. And, because the person element is the only thing specified for the folks element, a person element is the only thing it can contain. Of course, the person element has a DTD definition of its own, but the content requirements of a person element are independent of the content requirements of the folks element.

Also in Listing 2.4, the person element must contain the three elements named name, phone, and email. And because there is no occurrence modifier (like the asterisk in the folks element), each of these three elements must appear exactly once. Also, because they're separated by commas, they must appear in exactly the order in which they appear in the DTD.

```
 <?xml version="1.0" standalone="yes"?>

<!DOCTYPE folks [
<!ELEMENT folks (person)*>
<!ELEMENT person (name, phone, email)>
<!ELEMENT name (#PCDATA)>
<!ELEMENT phone (#PCDATA)>
<!ELEMENT email (#PCDATA)>
]>

<folks>
    <person>
        <name>Bertha D. Blues</name>
        <phone>907 555-8901</phone>
        <email>bertha@xyz.net</email>
    </person>
    <person>
        <name>Fred Drew</name>
        <phone>907 555-9921</phone>
        <email>fred@xyz.net</email>
    </person>
</folks>
```

Listing 2.4   An XML Document with a DTD

The elements name, phone, and email are specified to contain #PCDATA. This means they can only contain *parse character* data. In other words, they can only contain a character string that does not contain any other elements. Because the character string is parsed, it may contain things like the character entities that are predefined as part of the XML language.

Multiple Files

The example in Listing 2.5 is the same as the one in Listing 2.4, except that the DTD is stored in a separate file. An advantage to using this approach is that a separate file makes it easy to create several documents based on the same DTD without having to duplicate the DTD in every document. An additional advantage is that if the recipient of a transmitted document already has a copy of the DTD, there's no need to send another one. In fact, because the DTD is only for syntax checking, an application knows how to read the contents of a document formatted by the rules of a DTD. Therefore, there is no need for the recipient to refer to the DTD at all unless, for some reason, the receiver of the document does not trust the sender to format it correctly. The only purpose of the DTD is to check the syntax of a document.

```
<?xml version="1.0" standalone="no"?>

<!DOCTYPE folks SYSTEM "SimpleDoc.dtd">

<folks>
    <person>
        <name>Bertha D. Blues</name>
        <phone>907 555-8901</phone>
        <email>bertha@xyz.net</email>
    </person>
    <person>
        <name>Fred Drew</name>
        <phone>907 555-9921</phone>
        <email>fred@xyz.net</email>
    </person>
</folks>
```

Listing 2.5   An XML Document with an External DTD

The DOCTYPE keyword still serves the same purpose as before, but this time the SYSTEM keyword is used to precede the name of the file containing the DTD specifications. The name of the DTD file is in the same directory as this XML file, is named SimpleDoc.dtd, and contains the content shown in Listing 2.6.

This file contains only the definitions that go inside the DOCTYPE block, but not the DOCTYPE declaration itself (DOCTYPE declarations are discussed in detail in the following sections of this chapter). It does, however, have an XML declaration at the top. Also, the DTD file must include the encoding because the content of the file is going to be read and analyzed by the parser, and the parser needs to know what encoding scheme is being used.

The DOCTYPE Inline Declaration

The DOCTYPE inline declaration is the simplest form of DOCTYPE included in the XML file, as demonstrated in Listing 2.4. This form of DOCTYPE includes all of the DTD

```
<?xml version="1.0" encoding="US-ASCII"?>

<!ELEMENT folks (person)*>
<!ELEMENT person (name, phone, email)>
<!ELEMENT name (#PCDATA)>
<!ELEMENT phone (#PCDATA)>
<!ELEMENT email (#PCDATA)>
```

Listing 2.6   A Simple DTD File

declarations directly inline as a part of the XML document. Its basic form is shown in the following example:

```
<!DOCTYPE folks [
<!ELEMENT folks (person)*>
    . . .
]>
```

All of the DTD declarations are included between the DOCTYPE opening and closing brackets. This can include any combination of ELEMENT, CDATA, ATTLIST, ENTITY, IGNORE, and INCLUDE. And, of course, there can be any number of comments intermixed with the DTD definitions.

The DOCTYPE SYSTEM Declaration

Using the SYSTEM keyword enables you to specify the name of a file with either a relative or absolute URI. The following is an example of using a relative URI to specify the location of a file named inhere.dtd that's in the same directory as the XML document:

```
<!DOCTYPE folks SYSTEM "inhere.dtd">
```

The following example, another relative URI, specifies the file named insub.dtd in a local subdirectory named diction:

```
<!DOCTYPE folks SYSTEM "diction/insub.dtd">
```

An absolute URI can be used to specify the address of a file anywhere on the Internet. The following example shows the URI of a DTD document named SimpleDoc.dtd that's stored and readily available on the Internet. This very simple technique can be used to make sure that everyone is using the same DTDs to define the formats of the same set of documents:

```
<!DOCTYPE folks SYSTEM "http://www.belugalake/xdox/SimpleDoc.dtd">
```

NOTE The URI string will accept both forward and backward slashes to accommodate the naming requirements of different operating systems.

It is possible to use a SYSTEM DTD and, at the same time, include some DTD modifications that apply to the local document. You can include any statement that could also be written directly into the existing DTD. That is, you cannot override and replace an existing definition, but you can add definitions to the DTD. For example, you can add a new attribute definition for an existing tag, as in Listing 2.7.

This example uses the same DTD file that was used in previous examples, but this time the phone element is modified by ATTLIST to add the option of specifying an extension attribute. Details of ATTLIST are described later in this chapter.

```
<?xml version="1.0" standalone="no"?>
<!DOCTYPE folks SYSTEM "SimpleDoc.dtd" [
<!ATTLIST phone extension CDATA #IMPLIED>
]>

<folks>
    <person>
        <name>Bertha D. Blues</name>
        <phone extension="409">907 555-8901</phone>
        <email>bertha@xyz.net</email>
        <fax>907 555-3333</fax>
    </person>
</folks>
```

Listing 2.7   Adding an Attribute Definition to an Existing DTD

The DOCTYPE PUBLIC Declaration

The PUBLIC keyword works somewhat like the SYSTEM keyword, but with something added. The intention of this form is that it be used with a standard DTD that's been published and made widely available. Not only does this form of the DTD specification have a location (as with SYSTEM), but it also has a name. At first glance the name may appear to be a URI, but it isn't. It's in a special format laid out as follows:

```
prefix//owner//description//language ID
```

If the *prefix* is ISO, the DTD is an approved ISO standard. If the prefix is +, the DTD is an approved standard, but it is not an ISO standard. If the prefix is -, the DTD is an ISO standard proposal that has not yet been approved. The *owner* is the name, or an acronym, identifying the owner of the DTD specification. The *description* is a brief description of the DTD. The *language ID* is a two-letter ISO 639 specification of the language of the DTD.

The name of the DTD comes before the URI that specifies its location. The following example specifies that the DTD is to be the strict version of the W3C definition of HTML version 4.01:

```
<?xml version="1.0" standalone="no" ?>

<!DOCTYPE HTML PUBLIC "-//W3C//DTD HTML 4.01//EN"
            "http://www.w3.org/TR/html4/strict.dtd">

<html>
<head>
    The heading of the XHTML page.
</head>
```

```
<body>
    The body of the XHTML page.
</body>
</html>
```

In this example the name specifies that the DTD is a proposed ISO standard owned by the W3C organization. The descriptive name of the DTD is DTD HTML 4.01 and the language is EN (English). Judging by the URI, it seems this DTD is a very strict implementation of the standard; there are other versions at the same site of both transitional and loose implementations.

Also, as you would expect, you can make local additions to the DTD using the same technique as described earlier for the SYSTEM declaration.

Comments

It doesn't matter whether the DTD text is in the same file or in a separate file; the format of comments is the same as in any other section of an XML document. A valid comment looks like this:

```
<!-- Comments in DTD are in the same format as the rest of XML-->
```

The ELEMENT Declaration

The ELEMENT keyword is used to define the form of a tag in the XML document. It specifies both the tag name of the tag and the form of the tag content. An element definition consists of the ELEMENT keyword, followed by the name of the tag, followed by the rule that determines the content of the element.

The ANY Element

The keyword ANY can be used when you wish to define the tag name of an element but leave all the formatting of element content unspecified. An element defined this way can include any text and other elements (as long as all included elements are also valid) between its opening and closing tags. For example, the following specifies that the tag named nolimit is declared to be completely free form:

```
<!ELEMENT nolimit ANY>
```

This means that, as long as the syntax is correct, anything goes. All of the following are valid nolimit elements:

```
<nolimit>Text is okay for an ANY</nolimit>
<nolimit></nolimit>
<nolimit/>
<nolimit>Embedding<nolimit>another</nolimit>tag is okay</nolimit>
```

The EMPTY *Element*

It is possible to specify that an element to contain no data by defining it this way:

```
<!ELEMENT hr EMPTY>
```

An empty element is one that contains no text and no other elements. The following examples show the two possible forms of an empty element:

```
<hr></hr>
<hr/>
```

Note that even though an empty element cannot contain data between the tags, it can still have attributes defined for it. Details on declaring and using attributes are described later in this chapter. The following is an example of defining and using an optional attribute with the hr element:

```
<!ELEMENT hr EMPTY>
<!ATTLIST hr style #IMPLIED>
. . .
<hr style="reversed"/>
```

An Element with Mixed Content

The mixed content element definition allows a free mixture of text with any of the listed XML tags. To specify that character text may be included between the tags of an element, the keyword #PCDATA can be used. The following example specifies that the element named textonly can only contain text:

```
<!ELEMENT textonly (#PCDATA)>
```

#PCDATA must be included in parentheses. The name PCDATA is short for parsed character data, so-called because the parser actually reads through the text to find embedded tags or entities. At the very least, the parser has to scan the text to find the closing tag. The textonly tag, however, does not allow for any embedded tags; it can only be used for text as follows:

```
<textonly>Now is the time</textonly>
```

If you wish to specify that the content can be text intermixed with tags, you can use the vertical bar to separate the items and add an asterisk at the end to specify that the items in the parentheses can each be repeated any number of times as shown in the following example:

```
<!ELEMENT textag (#PCDATA | hr)*>
```

An element of the type textag can contain text with an unlimited number of hr elements embedded in it. You can extend this format to specify any number of element names that can be embedded in the text by listing them this way:

```
<!ELEMENT textags (#PCDATA | hr | b | br | bold | italic)*>
```

The vertical bars between the items indicates that the content can be any one of the items, and the asterisk at the end indicates that the item can be repeated any number of times. The result is that the content can be any amount of text with the named elements embedded in it any order.

An Element with Element Content

An element that contains only other elements is referred to as having *element content*. By using parentheses and the operators that specify the number of times each element is to occur, it's possible to specify any desired pattern of elements. The following example specifies that the content of the element pkone can be any one of three elements:

```
<!ELEMENT name (#PCDATA)>
<!ELEMENT address (#PCDATA)>
<!ELEMENT phone (#PCDATA)>
<!ELEMENT email (#PCDATA)>
<!ELEMENT pkone (name | address | phone)>
```

The vertical bar between two elements is the OR operator, and it indicates that one or the other may be used, but not both. As you can see, the OR operator can be used in a sequence specifying that only one of the members of the list can be selected. The following example specifies that the content of pkall must be all three of the named elements:

```
<!ELEMENT pkall (name , address , phone)>
```

A comma between two elements is an AND operator, which indicates that both elements must be included, and they must be included in the order in which they are listed. The pkall element must include the elements name, address, and phone, and they must appear in that order. The following examples demonstrate how these two forms can be combined to create a more complicated rule:

```
<!ELEMENT pkchoose (name, address, (phone | email))>
```

Using these element definitions, the following elements are valid:

```
<pkone>
    <name>Fred Drew</name>
</pkone>
<pkone>
    <phone>555-1028</phone>
</pkone>
<pkall>
    <name>Fred Drew</name>
    <address>1313 Luck St</address>
    <phone>555-1028</phone>
```

```
    </pkall>
    <pkchoose>
        <name>Fred Drew</name>
        <address>1313 Luck St</address>
        <phone>555-1028</phone>
    </pkchoose>
    <pkchoose>
        <name>Quintus Drew</name>
        <address>1315 Luck St</address>
        <email>quintus@homernet.net</email>
    </pkchoose>
```

The operators listed in Table 2.3 specify how often an item may be repeated. For example, the following definition specifies that the email address is optional, but there must be at least one (and possibly more) phone number:

```
<!ELEMENT contact (name , email? , phone+)>
```

The occurrence operators can also be applied to sets of items in parentheses. For example, the following specifies that a chlist element can contain any number of names and addresses. Each name and address must be accompanied by at least one phone or email element but can have any number of phone and email elements:

```
<!ELEMENT chlist (name, address, (phone | email)+)*>
```

The ATTLIST Declaration

The ATTLIST keyword can be used to specify one or more attributes that can be used as part of an element. This is done by specifying the element name, the name of the new attribute, and some rules about the value that can be assigned to the attribute. For example, for an element named rectangle to have a couple of attributes, they could be defined in the DTD as follows:

```
<!ELEMENT rectangle EMPTY>
<!ATTLIST rectangle height CDATA #IMPLIED>
<!ATTLIST rectangle width CDATA #IMPLIED>
```

Table 2.3 The Occurrence Operators

OPERATOR	DESCRIPTION
?	The item may be omitted but, if included, it can only appear once.
*	The item may be omitted and, if included, it can be repeated any number of times.
+	The item must be included at least once, and it may be repeated any number of times.
none	The item must be included once.

A single `ATTLIST` entry can also be used to declare multiple tags for the same element. An example is:

```
<!ELEMENT rectangle EMPTY>
<!ATTLIST rectangle height CDATA #IMPLIED
                    width CDATA #IMPLIED>
```

In the XML code, a valid `rectangle` element is required to include the two attributes declared with it, and it could look like this:

```
<rectangle width="100" height="200"/>
```

When defining an attribute, it's necessary to specify the data type and, possibly, an initial value or set of possible values. Table 2.4 lists the possible default declarations used to specify the requirement, or lack of requirement, imposed on attributes. Table 2.5 describes the keywords used to specify the type of data and gives an example of each one.

The `ENTITY` Declaration

An `ENTITY` declaration can be used to define textual substitution that will be made by the parser. If, for example, you wanted to insert a company name automatically throughout a document, you could do so by using the entity `&company;` you could define it as follows:

```
<!ENTITY company "International Widget Inc.">
```

The entity definition cannot be made inside an element, so it must come before the root element of the document. Once this entity has been defined, the string "International Widget Inc." will be inserted automatically wherever you use the entity, such as:

```
<customer>&company;</customer>
```

You can define a number of entities in a single document and use them to generalize the contents of the document itself. That is, by just changing the values of the entities, the content of the document would change. Just as was done with the predefined

Table 2.4 Declaring Validity Constraints of an Attribute

CONSTRAINT	DESCRIPTION
#IMPLIED	The attribute may used in an element of this type, but it is not required.
#REQUIRED	This attributed must be specified for all elements of this type.
#FIXED	This is always followed by a quoted string that is the only value that can be assigned to the attribute.

Table 2.5 Attribute Types

TYPE	DESCRIPTION	EXAMPLE

CDATA	If the attribute is specified in an element, its value can be any quoted string.	`<!ATTLIST elename altname`
		`  CDATA #REQUIRED>`
		`<elename altname="fred"/>`

ID	The name can be used as the target of a link from an IDREF of another element inside the document. In the future, this could also be a target for links from outside the document. An ID must be declared as either #IMPLIED or #REQUIRED. An element can only have one ID defined for it.	`<!ATTLIST locdef id`
		`  ID #IMPLIED>`
		`<locdef id="id8801"/>`

IDREF	This is the link from this element to an element with an ID attribute. The value provided for this tag makes the link by matching the value specified on an ID tag somewhere else in this document.	`<!ATTLIST locref taglink`
		`  IDREF #IMPLIED>`
		`<locref taglink="id8801"/>`

IDREFS	This is the same as IDREF except that it can be used to specify multiple references.	`<!ATTLIST locref taglink`
		`  IDREFS #IMPLIED>`
		`<locref taglink="id8801 id6422`
		`  id4733"/>`

ENTITY	The value must match an unparsed entity declared somewhere in the DTD. An unparsed entity is created by a NOTATION declaration.	`<!ATTLIST picture img`
		`  ENTITY #REQUIRED>`
		`<picture img="front"/>`

ENTITIES	The same as ENTITY except that it can be used to match multiple unparsed entities.	`<!ATTLIST picture img`
		`  ENTITIES #REQUIRED>`
		`<picture img="front back side`
		`  top"/>`

NMTOKEN	The value must be a valid name made up of letters, digits, periods, hyphens, and underscores. It may even contain a colon. It purpose is to simply specify a name.	`<!ATTLIST ident name`
		`  NMTOKEN #REQUIRED>`
		`<ident name="eggplant"/>`

NMTOKENS	This is the same as NMTOKEN except that it can specify a list of names.	`<!ATTLIST ident namelist`
		`  NMTOKENS #REQUIRED>`
		`<ident namelist="eggplant`
		`  grunion raspberry"/>`

```
<?xml version="1.0"?>

<!ENTITY company "International Widget Inc.">
<!ENTITY address "896 Grand Parkway">

<agreement>
  <intro>
    The company name is &company; with main offices
    located at &address;.
  </intro>
</agreement>
```

Listing 2.8   A Document Defining and Using Entities

entities, you can mix your own entities with text. The document in Listing 2.8 includes the definition of some entities and some text with a pair of entities embedded in it.

An even more generalized treatment of form of ENTITY is to store the substitution text in a separate file. By doing so, you'll need only to change the content of the entity file to make a modification to the document. This is done using the keyword SYSTEM as in the following:

```
<!ENTITY company SYSTEM "companyName.txt">
```

Just as with the SYSTEM keyword in the DOCTYPE declaration, the file can be located anywhere on the Internet.

Parameter Entities

A *parameter entity* can be used to make substitutions in the DTD instead of in the XML document. A normal entity does not cause substitutions to be made inside the DTD, so there's no way for the parser to recognize any of the DTD keywords. For example, the following will *not* work:

```
<!ENTITY cdreq "CDATA #REQUIRED">
<!ELEMENT post ANY>
<!ATTLIST post height &cdreq;>    <!-- Error -->
```

A parameter entry can be used to make the substitution work inside the DTD. To create a parameter entity, you'll need to insert a percent sign in front of the name of the entity being defined. An example is:

```
<!ENTITY % cdreq "CDATA #REQUIRED">
<!ELEMENT post ANY>
<!ATTLIST post height %cdreq;>
```

One place a parameter entity can be useful is where you'd otherwise need to repeat the same settings for several DTD entries. For example, several tags could have the same attribute defined for them as follows:

```
<!ATTLIST box visibility "(opaque|clear|translucent|red|green|blue)">
<!ATTLIST circle visibility "(opaque|clear|translucent|red|green|blue)">
<!ATTLIST diamond visibility
"(opaque|clear|translucent|red|green|blue)">
```

The same list of options could be defined as a parameter entity in a single place as follows:

```
<!ENTITY % visops "(opaque|clear|translucent|red|green|blue)">
<!ATTLIST box visibility %visops;>
<!ATTLIST circle visibility %visops;>
<!ATTLIST diamond visibility %visops;>
```

The advantage of using this technique is that you can make a change or a correction in only one place and have the change apply across all documents using the DTD.

Unparsed Entities

An unparsed entity is the mechanism by which a DTD creates pointers to data stored outside of the XML document. This data could include graphics, audio files, video, or other data not in a textual format. The term *unparsed* is used for this entity because it doesn't have to be in a well-formed XML format.

A few steps need to be taken to create a pointer to unparsed data. The first step is to declare a NOTATION entry that specifies a name for the format of the data. For example, the following statement in the DTD creates a NOTATION entry that refers to JPEG data:

```
<!NOTATION jpeg PUBLIC "JPEG">
```

The second step is to define the specific entity. The ENTITY statement uses the name of the format definition created in the NOTATION statement and specifies the physical location of the data. In fact, now that the data type has been established, you can use it as the basis for specifying a number of entities. The result of the ENTITY declarations in the following example is that the data is both located and named:

```
<!ENTITY Iliamna SYSTEM "http://www.belugalake.com/xdox/iliamna.jpeg"
        NDATA jpeg>
<!ENTITY Redoubt SYSTEM "http://www.belugalake.com/xdox/redoubt.jpeg"
        NDATA jpeg>
```

Now that the entity has been located and named, the third step is to add the ability to refer to the entity from an element. The element, and the attribute that will refer to the entity, are defined as follows:

```
<!ELEMENT picture (#PCDATA)>
<!ATTLIST picture img ENTITY #REQUIRED>
```

With all of these steps taken inside the DTD, the element can be used to refer directly to the data. For example, the two graphic files can be referred to as follows:

```
<gallery>
    <picture img="Iliamna">The Volcano Iliamna</picture>
    <picture img="Redoubt">The Volcano Redoubt</picture>
</gallery>
```

As with all XML documents, what happens to the data is in the hands of the program that processes the document, but it's perfectly reasonable to expect that some process will be able to display the pictures along with the supplied caption text.

The PI Declaration

A PI is an instruction or a set of instructions that are intended to be used by a process reading the XML document. The PI's content must be understood by both the author of the XML document and the process that reads the document. A PI can be intended for one specific process, so any other process can ignore it if it doesn't understand the content of the PI. For example, if an XML document is being used as a source of data to be stored in a file, the database process can ignore any instructions pertaining to displaying the data.

In the XML file, a processing instruction begins with `<?` and ends with `?>`. Its content consists of its name and one or more attribute named values. For example, if you wished to include information specifying the optimum size of a scrolled window to display the text, you could do that with the following PI:

```
<?scrollwin height="34" width="72"?>
```

The name of this PI is `scrollwin`, and it contains the two named data items, `height` and `width`.

The `scrollwin` PI data in the previous example could be used by a process as an aid for displaying data. This same information could, of course, be included as an attribute of one of the elements or even as text within an element, but it isn't really part of the data contained by the document. There is no need to burden the document formatting with special elements and attributes when the purpose is simply to pass instructions to a single process that may or may not be the recipient of the document.

> **NOTE** The first line of an XML document is a PI that specifies the XML version number. It is a very special PI because it's named *xml*, and this name is known to the parser that reads the document. The two pieces of information it contains, named *version* and *standalone*, are also known to the parser. Although it's possible for an application reading an XML document to also read the *xml* PI, there's seldom any need for it to do so.

Conditional Inclusion with `IGNORE` and `INCLUDE`

The keywords `IGNORE` and `INCLUDE` inside a DTD make it possible for a section of code to be ignored or included by the parser during processing. The following example illustrates how to have the parser ignore a section of code:

```
<![IGNORE[
 . . .
]]>
```

Similarly, the following example will allow the specified section to be read and parsed normally:

```
<![INCLUDE[
 . . .
]]>
```

The syntax is the same for both of these, so it's possible to include or exclude sections of the DTD by simply changing the name from `IGNORE` to `INCLUDE` or vice versa. Specifying `IGNORE` has the same effect as enclosing the section between a `<!--` and a `-->`, making it into a comment. Switching to `INCLUDE` has the same effect as removing the comment marks.

You can control the inclusion by using an entity like the following, which could be used to toggle several sections on and off:

```
<!ENTITY % onoff "INCLUDE">
<![%onoff;[
 . . .
]]>
```

Namespaces

XML namespaces are used to help make certain that element names are unique. A name defined as a member of a namespace is made up of two parts. The first part is the prefix and is the same for all names in the same space. The second part is the name itself and is unique within its namespace. The two parts are joined by a colon. The following are some examples of names specified with their namespaces:

```
Customer:name
Customer:address
Company:name
Company:address
Company:phone
```

There are two namespaces in these examples—one is `Customer` and the other is `Company`. Even though name and address are both repeated, each is in its own namespace, making each one distinct.

A namespace used inside an XML document is completely unique. This is achieved by the namespace name inside a document being a universally unique string. Any string can be used for this purpose, but to guarantee uniqueness, a namespace inside an XML document is associated with a URI. For example, the Web site for this book is http://www.belugalake.com/xbox, so to create a completely unique name, this URL could be used as the basis of the unique identifying string. There is nothing in particular stored at the address; it's used strictly as a method of guaranteeing uniqueness. The namespace name in this example is to be `Customer`, and the URI it is to be associated with is `http://www.belugalake.com/xbox/custspace`; then the name is associated with its URI in the opening tag of the root element, as follows:

```
<folks xmlns:Customer="http://www.belugalake.com/xbox/custspace">
```

The name `Customer` is simply for convenience; it's a simple name internal to the XML document used to represent the URI string. Also, for all practical purposes, in XML a URI and a URL can be treated identically because all characters following the appearance of a hash character are ignored by XML. It often happens that a URL further qualifies its target by appending a hash character and adding more information; this never occurs with a URI.

Namespaces were not part of the original XML specification; they're specified in a separate document. The DTD is unaware of namespaces, so you have to specify the setting as an attribute for the root element. Specifying each tag name with a colon is no problem for the DTD because XML has always allowed colons in names.

The namespace specification occurs, in the form of an attribute, in the opening tag of the root element. The attribute specifying the namespace is written with the prefix `xmlns`, which stands for XML Namespace, followed by a colon and the namespace name. The name `xmlns` is one of the names that XML reserves for its own use—recall that any name beginning with any case combination of the letters xml is reserved for internal use.

A Simple Namespace

To establish a namespace for an XML document, name it in the root element and then use it with the element tags inside the document. Listing 2.9 is an example of a docu-

```
<?xml version="1.0" standalone="yes"?>
<contacts:folks xmlns:contacts="www.belugalake.com/xbox/contacts">
    <contacts:person>
        <contacts:name>Bertha D. Blues</contacts:name>
        <contacts:phone>907 555-8901</contacts:phone>
        <contacts:email>bertha@xyz.net</contacts:email>
    </contacts:person>
</contacts:folks>
```

Listing 2.9 A Simple Namespace Declaration

```
<?xml version="1.0" standalone="yes"?>
<folks xmlns="www.belugalake.com/xbox/contacts">
    <person>
        <name>Bertha D. Blues</name>
        <phone>907 555-8901</phone>
        <email>bertha@xyz.net</email>
    </person>
</folks>
```

Listing 2.10   A Simple Namespace Set as the Default

ment with the root element defining the namespace and the namespace being included as part of the tag names.

It is important to remember that it's the string (normally a URI) that uniquely identifies the namespace, not the name used in the XML. The internal name is used only as a notational convenience. The document in Listing 2.9 could have used the internal name "leads" instead of "contacts," but by specifying the URI, it would be the same namespace.

The Default Namespace

If you're using only one namespace, and every element in the document is in the same namespace, you can declare a default namespace that has no local name. That is, in Listing 2.9, the name "contacts" was used to identify the namespace internally, but if there is no conflict, it is not necessary to do so. Listing 2.10 uses the same namespace as Listing 2.9 because it uses the same URI, but in this case, there's no internal name assigned to the namespace, so there's no need to use one on every tag.

Normally the default namespace will automatically apply to every tag name inside the one in which it's specified, but it's possible to shield some tags from the default. In Listing 2.11 the default namespace will be applied to `folks`, `person`, and `name` but will not be applied to `reach`, `phone`, and `email`.

```
<?xml version="1.0" standalone="yes"?>
<folks xmlns="www.belugalake.com/xobx/defltspc">
    <person>
        <name>Bertha D. Blues</name>
        <reach xmlns="">
            <phone>907 555-8901</phone>
            <email>bertha@xyz.net</email>
        </reach>
    </person>
</folks>
```

Listing 2.11   Overriding the Default Namespace

```
<?xml version="1.0" standalone="yes"?>
<contacts:folks xmlns:contacts="www.belugalake.com/xbox/contacts"
          xmlns:ident="www.belugalake.com/xbox/ndts"
          xmlns="http://www.homernet.net/medlxt">
    <contacts:person>
        <ident:name>Bertha D. Blues</ident:name>
        <phone>907 555-8901</phone>
        <email>bertha@xyz.net</email>
    </contacts:person>
    <contacts:person>
        <ident:name>Fred Drew</ident:name>
        <phone>907 555-9921</phone>
        <email>fred@xyz.net</email>
    </contacts:person>
</contacts:folks>
```

Listing 2.12   Multiple Namespaces with a Default

Multiple Namespaces

It is possible to define multiple namespaces and intermix the tags from each of these spaces. It's even possible to use one of them as the default namespace. Listing 2.12 uses three different namespaces, one of which is the default.

In Listing 2.12, the tags named folks and person are in the namespace associated with "www.belugalake.com/xbox/contacts". The name tag is in the namespace associated with "www.belugalake.com/xbox/ndts". The tags phone and email, which are not prefixed by a specific namespace, fall into the default namespace that's associated with "http://www.homernet.net/medlxt".

A Namespace Defined in a DTD

The XML document in Listing 2.13 demonstrates how to set up and use a namespace.

The DTD that defines a namespace must use the full name of the tags in the element syntax definitions. Other than that, there is no real difference in the DTD. Every namespace name is defined as a part of the root element and uses a URI string as its identifier to guarantee that the namespace is unique. The content at the URI location is never used; it is only the URI itself that is used to test for uniqueness.

```
<?xml version="1.0" standalone="yes"?>

<!DOCTYPE Directory:folks [
<!ELEMENT Directory:folks (Directory:person)*>
<!ATTLIST Directory:folks xmlns:Directory CDATA #REQUIRED>
<!ELEMENT Directory:person
        (Directory:name, Directory:phone, Directory:email)>
<!ELEMENT Directory:name (#PCDATA)>
<!ELEMENT Directory:phone (#PCDATA)>
<!ELEMENT Directory:email (#PCDATA)>
]>

<Directory:folks xmlns:Directory="www.belugalake.com/xbox">
    <Directory:person>
        <Directory:name>Bertha D. Blues</Directory:name>
        <Directory:phone>907 555-8901</Directory:phone>
        <Directory:email>bertha@xyz.net</Directory:email>
    </Directory:person>
    <Directory:person>
        <Directory:name>Fred Drew</Directory:name>
        <Directory:phone>907 555-9921</Directory:phone>
        <Directory:email>fred@xyz.net</Directory:email>
    </Directory:person>
</Directory:folks>
```

Listing 2.13   A Typical Approach for Defining and Using a Namespace

Multiple Namespaces in a DTD

It's possible to use more than one namespace in an XML document. The example in Listing 2.14 is a modification of Listing 2.13, where all the tag names were in the Directory namespace. In this example, the tags for phone and email have been defined as being in the Com namespace.

In the XML document, the root element Directory:folks is used to specify the URI associated with both namespaces. A well-formed document may have any number of namespaces. For it to be a valid document, each of the namespaces must be specified as being an attribute of the root element.

```
<?xml version="1.0" standalone="yes"?>

<!DOCTYPE Directory:folks [
<!ELEMENT Directory:folks (Directory:person)*>
<!ATTLIST Directory:folks xmlns:Directory CDATA #REQUIRED>
<!ATTLIST Directory:folks xmlns:Com CDATA #REQUIRED>
<!ELEMENT Directory:person
        (Directory:name, Com:phone, Com:email)>
<!ELEMENT Directory:name (#PCDATA)>
<!ELEMENT Com:phone (#PCDATA)>
<!ELEMENT Com:email (#PCDATA)>
]>

<Directory:folks xmlns:Directory="www.belugalake.com/xbox"
            xmlns:Com="www.alphabetic.info">
    <Directory:person>
        <Directory:name>Bertha D. Blues</Directory:name>
        <Com:phone>907 555-8901</Com:phone>
        <Com:email>bertha@xyz.net</Com:email>
    </Directory:person>
    <Directory:person>
        <Directory:name>Fred Drew</Directory:name>
        <Com:phone>907 555-9921</Com:phone>
        <Com:email>fred@xyz.net</Com:email>
    </Directory:person>
</Directory:folks>
```

Listing 2.14   Defining Two Namespaces in One DTD

Summary

This chapter, by describing the syntax of XML, lays a foundation for the information that is presented in all the remaining chapters of the book. I suspect that as you proceed through the chapters on writing programs to read and process XML documents, and the sections on invoking the methods to check and validate incoming documents, you may need to refer to this chapter from time to time. For that reason, every attempt was made to organize the chapter logically, with clear headings, and to keep things to a bare minimum so, it is hoped, it will be easy to find things.

Fortunately, the syntax is really not as arcane as it first appears when you just read through it. As you get an overview of the two JAXP parsers in Chapter 3, and then see how XML is processed in the chapters that follow, the logic behind the syntax of an XML document should become clear. I think you will discover that XML syntax and processing are really quite clever.

CHAPTER

3

SAX and DOM in the JAXP

This chapter discusses the basic tools available for reading XML documents into your program and includes a comparative description of the two approaches to parsing XML documents. Both approaches are available in the JAXP, so it's up to you and your application to decide which one you want to use; each has its own set of advantages and disadvantages. The purpose of an XML parser is to read a document and provide your application with its content so that it can find the pieces of the document it is to process. When choosing which parser approach to take, you have to consider what you need from the document and what you intend to do with it when you've got it.

The SAX Parser

The SAX parser reads an XML document and passes the document pieces to your application one at a time, in the same order they appear in the document. In other words, the SAX parser reads the document sequentially and breaks it into components. This is known as *event-based* parsing because, conceptually, as the parser reads through the document, each individual piece is extracted and reported to the application through a callback method that you've devised and included in your application. The type of input data determines which method is called. For example, the following is a very simple XML document:

```
<?xml version="1.0"?>
<simpledoc>
    <stmt>
        A line of text.
    </stmt>
</simpledoc>
```

The SAX parser will read this document and report the following series of events, in this order, to your application:

```
start document
start element: simpledoc
start element: stmt
text: "A line of text."
end element: stmt
end element: simpledoc
end document
```

Nothing is stored in the parser. Once the last event is reported to your application, you will not hear from the parser again and you cannot query it for information. You can think of SAX as simply a lexical scanner that is used to tokenize the input XML document and feed the tokens to your program as they appear. While SAX is called a parser, there is no precedence processing or any other form of processing involved. As simple as it is, it has many uses, some of which are explored in Chapters 4 and 5.

SAX 1.0 and SAX 2.0

There are two versions of SAX, commonly referred to as SAX1 and SAX2. SAX1 is the original API specification that stabilized in 1998. Limitations were later discovered, so SAX2 was created as an extension of SAX1. SAX2 does everything SAX1 does but is also capable of handling things that SAX1 couldn't, like namespaces and external entities.

The JAXP has been designed in such a way that it works with both SAX1 and SAX2, and this caused some parts of the API design to be less straightforward than it would have been otherwise. The API is well designed—it all works correctly—it's just that there were some style decisions that may appear odd. If you want to see an example (probably the most obvious example), take a look at the first example program in Chapter 4 to see how the XMLParser and XMLReader are handled.

This book does not differentiate between SAX1 and SAX2, but the examples are based on the capabilities of SAX2 because it can do everything SAX1 can do, and a bit more.

The Definition of SAX

There is no official specification for SAX in the traditional sense. It was originally defined, and continues to be defined, as a set of documented Java interfaces and classes. It is free and open and has even been implemented in other languages. There are working versions in Perl, Python, C++, and probably some other languages as well. There are also some versions in Java that have included extensions to serve special purposes. If you want to explore the wide world of SAX parsers, take a look at the following Web site: www.megginson.com/SAX/index.html

SAX is defined as two Java packages. The package `org.xml.sax` listed in Table 3.1 is the one used most often by applications. The classes defined in the package `org.xml.sax.helpers` shown in Table 3.2 contains classes and interfaces that can also be used directly in an application to take care of special circumstances where an

Table 3.1   The `org.xml.sax` Package

NAME	DESCRIPTION
AttributeList	Deprecated. Use `AttributesAttributes` An interface for a class capable of containing a list of XML attribute names and values.
ContentHandler	An interface that defines methods to receive notification of XML events from the parser. This is the main interface implemented by most applications.
DocumentHandler	Deprecated. Use `ContentHandler`.
DTDHandler	An interface that defines methods to receive notification of DTD events from the parser.
EntityResolver	A class implementing this interface can act as an agent of the XML reader for resolving entity references.
ErrorHandler	An interface that defines the methods to receive the different kinds of error messages issued by the parser.
HandlerBase	Deprecated. Use `DefaultHandler` in the `org.xml.sax.helpers` package.
InputSource	A class that can be used to encapsulate a single XML document for input.
Locator	An interface for the container of the specification of a location in an XML source document.
Parser	Deprecated. Use `XMLReader`.
SAXException	The exception thrown for a general SAX error and the base class of the other parser errors.

(continues)

Table 3.1 (*continued*)

NAME	DESCRIPTION
SAXNotRecognizedException	The exception thrown on encountering an unrecognized feature or property identifier in the input.
SAXNotSupportedException	The exception thrown on encountering a recognized, but unsupported, feature or property identifier in the input.
SAXParseException	The exception thrown for a SAX syntax or other parse error.
XMLFilter	An extension of the XMLReader interface to add the capability of using another XMLReader for input, which enables the construction of a filter that may be inserted into the input stream of events being sent to the application
XMLReader	An interface that defines methods used for reading and parsing an XML document.

Table 3.2   The org.xml.sax.helper Package

NAME	DESCRIPTION
AttributeListImpl	Deprecated. Use AttributresImpl.
AttributesImpl	A class that is the default implementation of the Attributes interface.
DefaultHandler	A convenience base class for SAX2 event handlers. It provides default implementations for the core SAX interfaces.
LocatorImpl	A convenience implementation of the Locator interface.
NamespaceSupport	A class that encapsulates namespace logic.
ParserAdapter	This class is a wrapper around a SAX1 parser so that it can be used as if it were a SAX2 parser.
ParserFactory	Deprecated. Use XMLReaderFactory.
XMLFilterImpl	A convenience base class for the creation of a filter that uses the XMLFilter interface.
XMLReaderAdapter	The class is a wrapper around a SAX2 parser so that it can be used as if it were a SAX1 parser.
XMLReaderFactory	A class that provides static methods used for the creation of XMLReader objects.

Table 3.3 The `org.xml.sax.ext` Package

NAME	DESCRIPTION
`DeclHandler`	An interface used in the optional extension enabling parsing of DTD declarations found in an XML document.
`LexicalHandler`	An interface used in the optional extension enabling the detection of normally unparsed items such as comments and CDATA sections.

application wants access to more than simply the results of the parse. The package `org.xml.sax.ext` listed in Table 3.3 defines interfaces used to implement extensions to SAX. There are some deprecated interfaces and classes shown in all of the tables. These deprecations were necessary modifications that were made to allow for a clean transition of the API from SAX1 to SAX2 and, at the same time, result in an API that successfully supports both versions of SAX. In effect, SAX1 is deprecated, but it can still be used, which means that any existing applications will still successfully compile and run.

There is one very important consequence of the names used to define the SAX interfaces and classes. Some of the names used are the same as the ones used in the core Java API. This makes it important *not* to use wildcards to import entire packages. For example, the following pair of import statements causes an ambiguity because both packages contain a `ContentHandler`:

```
import java.net.*;        // wrong
import org.xml.sax.*;     // wrong
```

It would be better to import the individual class and interfaces by their full names, as in the following:

```
import java.net.URL;
import java.net.Socket;
import org.xml.sax.ContentHandler;
```

This not only clears up the ambiguity, but it also makes for a somewhat cleaner and clearer source file. If you wind up in the situation where you need the `ContentHandler` from both packages, you'll simply have to omit the import statements and use its full name in the code. After all, the only real purpose of the import statement is for the convenience of using shorter names in the code.

The DOM Parser

Unlike SAX, the DOM specification is independent of the Java language. In fact, it's designed so that it can be implemented in any programming language. Its specification is that of a set of objects that can be used to dynamically access and update the content and structure of a document. At least that was the intention of the writers of the specification. As you read the specification, however, it's very difficult not to think of it in terms of Java classes, interfaces, and objects.

The DOM specification defines a set of objects. Each specified object type can contain information of a certain type that can be found in an XML document. Each object provides methods that allow the data from the document to be accessed and manipulated. There are also methods for defining the relationships among the objects to represent the organization of the document. Using these objects, an application can move freely from one place to another in a document to extract data and to make any desired changes.

A DOM parser does nothing more than read the XML documents and organize the document content into a memory-resident collection of objects representing the original document. The result is a parse tree with the object at the root of the tree representing the entire document. An application can then navigate freely through the branches of the tree and manipulate the contents of the document (by modifying the contents of a tree node) and manipulate the shape of the document itself (by deleting and inserting tree nodes).

To demonstrate the organization of a DOM parse tree, the following simple XML document is diagrammed:

```
<?xml version="1.0"?>
<simpledoc>
    <stmt>A line of text</stmt>
    <stmt>A <bold>second</bold>line of text</stmt>
</simpledoc>
```

Parsing this document into a memory-resident tree results in the document being stored in a tree organized like the one diagrammed in Figure 3.1

The DOM Specification

The DOM specification originated with the World Wide Web Consortium (W3C). Unlike SAX, DOM was not designed specifically for use with Java; instead DOM is specified as a general processing definition that can be used with any programming language. If you would like to read or download a copy of the specification, it can be found at the following Web site: http://www.w3.org/TR/REC-DOM-Level-1/. If you want general information about DOM, including the history and current activities, use the following link: http://www.w3.org/DOM.

The DOM specification is a work in progress with Level 1 being only the foundation document for development of higher-level specifications. The level 1 specification is constantly being extended by changes in the levels above it. Level 1 is relatively stable and unchanging, whereas the other levels are being modified and expanded. The levels are as follows:

1. Level 1 is the core of DOM. It contains the fundamentals necessary for document navigation and manipulation.

2. Level 2 includes a stylesheet object model and provides methods of modifying the document style. It also provides the ability to access tree members by namespace names.

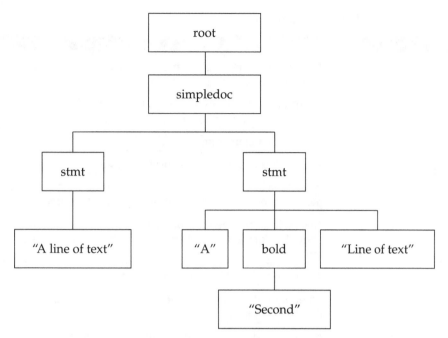

Figure 3.1   The Organization of a Simple DOM Parse Tree

3. Level 3 deals with the process of reading an XML document into a memory-resident tree as well as the reverse action of writing a tree to an XML document or even to some other format.

4. Level 4 (and possibly further levels) addresses windowing or other interfaces. This level involves capabilities such as formatting data for display and prompting the user for input and could also include a query language interface, multi-threading, security, and so on.

The DOM that is in use today is based on the first three levels. The development of the higher levels (4 and above) of the specification are proceeding, but there is nothing of real substance as yet. The details of the implementation of the first three levels are explored in detail, with working examples, in Chapters 6, 7, and 8. In place of using the DOM specification for display, XML documents are quite often converted into HTML and displayed in a Web browser.

The scope and purpose of DOM changed somewhat as the specifications were being written. DOM originally was conceived as a technique for allowing JavaScript and Java programs to be portable among Web browsers. The starting point for DOM was the concept of dynamic HTML, that is, HTML documents being automatically generated when a request to view a page arrived at a Web server. As the specification process proceeded, influence from SGML entered the process, which resulted in the object model on which DOM is based. As it now stands, the XML data storage format (which is much closer to SGML than is HTML) has become more important than the intended end product.

Table 3.4   DOM Objects That Make Up the Parse Tree

NAME	DESCRIPTION
Attr	An attribute consisting of a name (sometimes called a key) and a value to be associated with the name.
CDATASection	A block of text in an escape format to allow for the inclusion of special characters. Otherwise it is the same as Text.
Comment	The text of a comment.
Document	The root node of the entire document tree.
DocumentFragment	A lightweight form of Document primarily used for editing a parse tree by extracting and inserting parts of the tree.
DocumentType	The node in the tree that contains descriptive information about the format of the elements (it is the schema or DTD information).
Element	A tag used to mark up a section of text.
Entity	An entity, either parsed or unparsed. This is the entity itself, not the declaration.
EntityReference	An unexpanded entity. A parser may choose to expand all entity references omitting objects of this type.
Notation	A notation declared as part of the DTD or schema. It is either an unparsed entity or processing instruction.
ProcessingInstruction	A processing instruction is a processor-specific instruction included in the document.
Text	Character data.

The DOM objects are defined in the specification by name. A collection of these objects, listed in Table 3.4, are used to hold the memory-resident form of an XML document. Each object represents a specific type of item from the document, and the relationships among the objects determine the exact order of their appearance in the document. The objects are organized in memory in the form of a tree. Each node of the tree has a parent node (except, of course, for Document root node of the tree), and each node may have one or more child nodes attached to it. An example of the organization of a parse tree is shown in Figure 3.1. There are only certain parent/child node relationships that can exist in the parse tree, and these are listed in Table 3.5.

The Notation object in Table 3.5 has no parent/child relationships defined for it because it's a special case. In addition to the Notation object, there are other circumstances where a relationship may be defined outside of the regular tree structure, but for the most part, the relationships follow the structure in Table 3.5. Probably the most notable exception is the Attr object, which has no parent; it is included in a special way as part of an Element object. These special cases are explored in the example program in Chapter 6 where the entire parse tree is listed.

Table 3.5 The DOM Objects with Parent/Child Relationships

NAME	PARENTS	CHILDREN
Attr	None	EntityReference, Text
CDATASection	DocumentFragment, Entity, EntityReference	None
Comment	Document, DocumentFragment, Entity, EntityReference	None
Document	None	Comment, DocumentType, Element, ProcessingInstruction, Text
DocumentFragment	None	CDATASection, Comment, Element, EntityReference, ProcessingInstruction, Text
DocumentType	Document	None
Element	Document, DocumentFragment, Entity, EntityReference	None
Entity	None	CDATASection, Comment, Element, EntityReference, ProcessingInstruction, Text
EntityReference	Attr, DocumentFragment, Entity, EntityReference	CDATASection, Comment, Element, EntityReference, ProcessingInstruction, Text
Notation	None	None
ProcessingInstruction	Document, DocumentFragment, Entity, EntityReference	None
Text	Attr, Document, DocumentFragment, Entity, EntityReference	None

DOM as a Java Package

The specification of the DOM parse tree is implemented in the JAXP as the package `org.w3c.dom` listed in Table 3.6. This package consists of a collection of interface definitions and one class named `DOMException`. The interfaces are nodes in a DOM parse tree. The `Node` interface is the general parse tree node type from which all of the other node types are extended. This automatically supplies each node in the tree with a standard set of methods that can be used by an application to move from one node to the next through the tree.

Table 3.6   The `org.w3c.dom` Package

NAME	DESCRIPTION
Attr	A parse tree node that contains a single attribute of an element.
CDATASection	A parse tree node that contains text that appears in the document as a CDATA section.
CharacterData	A parse tree node that contains text. Its purpose is to be the super-interface of the CDATASection, Comment, and Text interfaces, all of which contain text.
Comment	A parse tree node that contains text that appears in the document as a comment.
Document	The root node of a parse tree that contains an entire document.
DocumentFragment	The root node of a subdocument, usually created by extracting a portion of a larger parse tree.
DocumentType	A parse tree node that contains the DTD information of a document.
DOMException	The exception thrown to indicate a severe error in processing.
DOMImplementation	An interface that defines methods that are independent of the document's parse tree.
Element	A parse tree node that contains an XML element.
Entity	A parse tree node that contains the definition of an entity of the document.
EntityReference	A parse tree node that contains a reference to an entity within the document text.
NamedNodeMap	An unordered collection of parse tree nodes that can be accessed by name.

Table 3.6 (*continued*)

NAME	DESCRIPTION
Node	The super-interface of all parse tree nodes.
NodeList	An ordered list of parse tree nodes that can be accessed by index.
Notation	A parse tree node that contains a notation declaration of the document's DTD.
ProcessingInstruction	A parse tree node that contains the name and text of a processing instruction.
Text	A parse tree node that contains the text of an element.

Some constant values are defined as part of the Java API. Table 3.7 lists the constants used as the error codes that specify the cause of a DOMException object being thrown. Table 3.8 lists the constants that are used in the parse tree to signify the node types. These are all defined as named constants and, as such, are subject to change in future releases of the software. Most of the actual values, however, are mentioned in conjunction with the DOM specification, so they are unlikely to be modified.

Table 3.7 The Error Codes of DOMException

NAME	VALUE	DESCRIPTION
DOMSTRING_SIZE_ERR	2	The specified range of text does not fit into a DOMString.
HIERARCHY_REQUEST_ERR	3	The insertion of the node would violate the relationships shown in Table 3.5.
INDEX_SIZE_ERR	1	An index value is either negative or beyond the last indexable member.
INUSE_ATTRIBUTE_ERR	10	The attribute being added is already in use elsewhere.
INVALID_ACCESS_ERR	15	The parameter, or the requested operation, is not supported by the underlying object.
INVALID_CHARACTER_ERR	5	An invalid character has been encountered in a name, or an unknown character has been encountered elsewhere.
INVALID_MODIFICATION_ERR	13	An attempt was made to modify the type of the underlying object.
INVALID_STATE_ERR	11	At attempt was made to use an object that is not usable.

(continues)

Table 3.7   (*continued*)

NAME	VALUE	DESCRIPTION
NAMESPACE_ERR	14	An attempt was made to create or change an object in a way that violates the namespace definitions.
NO_DATA_ALLOWED_ERR	6	Data was specified for a node that cannot contain data.
NO_MODIFICATION_ ALLOWED_ERR	7	An attempt was made to modify a node where modifications are not allowed.
NOT_FOUND_ERR	8	The node does not exist in the context in which it was referenced.
NOT_SUPPORTED_ERR	9	This implementation does not support either the object type or the requested operation.
SYNTAX_ERR	12	An invalid or illegal string has been specified.
WRONG_DOCUMENT_ERR	4	An attempt was made to use a node in a document other than the one in which it was created.

Table 3.8   The Constants Specifying the Parse Tree Node Types

NAME	VALUE
ATTRIBUTE_NODE	2
CDATA_SECTION_NODE	4
COMMENT_NODE	8
DOCUMENT_FRAGMENT_NODE	11
DOCUMENT_NODE	9
DOCUMENT_TYPE_NODE	10
ELEMENT_NODE	1
ENTITY_NODE	6
ENTITY_REFERENCE_NODE	5
NOTATION_NODE	12
PROCESSING_INSTRUCTION_NODE	7
TEXT_NODE	3

Table 3.9   The `javax.xml.parsers` Package

NAME	DESCRIPTION
`DocumentBuilder`	A DOM parser class capable of reading an XML document and storing it in a parse tree
`DocumentBuilderFactory`	A factory class that creates objects of the DocumentBuilder class
`FactoryConfigurationError`	An error thrown to indicate a configuration error in a parser factory
`ParserConfigurationException`	An exception thrown to indicate a configuration error in a parser
`SAXParser`	A SAX parser class capable of reading an XML document and reporting the events to an application
`SAXParserFactory`	A factory class that creates objects of the SAXParser class

The Rest of JAXP

A complete implementation of both SAX and DOM are included as part of the JAXP and, in addition, there are a number of other classes that can be used to facilitate the use of both SAX and DOM in an application. The resulting collection of packages makes it a relatively straightforward procedure to construct an application that is capable of processing XML documents. In particular, beyond the fundamentals of DOM and SAX parsing, there are classes and interfaces that can be used to manage the process of transforming an XML document.

The package `javax.xml.parsers` listed in Table 3.9 contains classes and methods for acquiring both DOM and SAX parsers. The package `java.xml.transform` listed in Table 3.10 defines a generic API that is neither SAX nor DOM and can used for document transformation. The package `javax.xml.transform.stream` in Table 3.11 contains classes used for document input and output during transformation. The package `javax.xml.tranform.dom` in Table 3.12 contains the DOM specific transformation utilities, and the package `javax.xml.transform.sax` in Table 3.13 contains the SAX specific transformation utilities.

Table 3.10 The `java.xml.transform` Package

NAME	DESCRIPTION
ErrorListener	An interface used by an application to customize the handling of parser errors
OutputKeys	A class providing string constants of output properties
Result	An interface for redirecting the output from a class that is building a transformation result tree
Source	An interface for redirecting the input of either an XML document or transformation instructions
SourceLocator	An interface that defines access to information on the location of an error in XML source or transformation instruction
Templates	An interface that provides access to internally stored executable transformation instructions
Transformer	A class that converts a source tree into a result tree
TransformerConfigurationException	An exception thrown to indicate a serious configuration error
TransformerException	An exception thrown to indicate an error during transformation
TransformerFactory	A factory class that produces Transformer and Template objects
TransformerFactoryConfigurationError	An exception thrown to indicate a configuration problem with a transformer factory
URIResolver	An interface for conversion of a `document()`, `xsl:import`, or `xsl:include` command into a `Source` object

Table 3.11   The `javax.xml.transform.stream` Package

NAME	DESCRIPTION
StreamResult	A class that buffers and streams the output of the transformation process
StreamSource	A class that streams the source XML document for transformation

Table 3.12   The `javax.xml.tranform.dom` Package

NAME	DESCRIPTION
DOMLocator	An interface that maps a parse tree node back to a location in the original document
DOMResult	A class that holds the DOM parse tree that results from a transformation
DOMSource	A class that holds the DOM parse tree that is the input to a transformation

Table 3.13   The `javax.xml.transform.sax` Package

NAME	DESCRIPTION
SAXResult	A class that holds a transformation result
SAXSource	A class that holds the source input to a transformation
SAXTransformerFactory	A factory class that produces factories to generate either `Transformers` or `Templates`
TemplatesHandler	An interface that extends `org.xml.sax.ContentHandler` to convert SAX incoming parse events into `javax.xml.transform.Templates` objects
TransformerHandler	An interface for listening to SAX parse events and transforming them into a `javax.xml.transform.Result` object

Summary

There are two parsers for an XML document, and they could not be more different. One is strictly a sequential token reader, and the other creates a memory-resident tree according to precedence. The sequential parse is not really specified; it is defined loosely as a set of Java interfaces, and many implementations add extensions of their own. The tree parse is specified in minute detail in a multilevel document by a standards organization. Although these two parsers are designed to perform the same basic function, they do so in very different ways.

All XML processing begins with using one of these parsers. The next four chapters explore different ways of using these two parsers in applications. The next chapter begins the process with examples of using a SAX parser to discover and list all the content found in an XML document.

SAX Document Parse and Read

This chapter discusses how application programs can use a SAX parser to parse XML documents. Two sample application programs are examined: One is named SAXCheck and the other is SAXDump. Both sample programs are as simple as possible, so the use of the JAXP API is clearly exposed instead of being obscured inside a complicated application. The first program demonstrates the code necessary for basic SAX parsing and how errors can be handled. The second does the same, but it also processes each piece of the XML document as it is returned from the parser.

How SAX Parsers Are Used

A SAX parser is very simple. It reads straight through the XML document and returns to your application each piece of the document as it is found. It is quick and efficient because it uses very little memory by not keeping track of anything it finds in the document, nor does it look ahead to resolve any references to things coming further down in the document. It just reads each piece and passes it on to your application. So your application must be prepared to process things in the same sequential way; you cannot use the parser to move from one place to another in the incoming parsed data. For an application that does not need to change the order of the data, a sequential read of the document is all that is necessary. For example, there is no need to implement complicated associations for a simple configuration file or some other document in which the XML is used simply to mark sections of the document for identification.

The SAX parser can also be used if you are writing an application to display a document in some format marked up by XML elements. The XML in that document would then be processed by the application in a manner similar to the way HTML is processed in a Web browser. It could be that a sequential read through the document is all you need. The SAX parser will break down each piece of the document and pass the pieces to your application sequentially and in a form that is easy for a program to handle.

The SAX parser would also be useful when you want to process an XML document to add, remove, or make changes to some elements. Perhaps all you need to do is be able to read straight through the document and make a change whenever you find a place where one belongs. The general term for this kind of processing is *filtering*. Because the SAX parser invokes the callback methods to pass, sequentially, all of the information found in the input document directly to the process, it is a simple matter for the process to turn around and output another complete document with whatever modifications you would like.

SAX Error Checking

The most fundamental action of a parser is the detection and reporting of error conditions. The SAX parser provides an interface named `ErrorHandler` that defines the set of methods used as callbacks to report parse errors to your application. The class in Listing 4.1 is an example of a program that implements the interface, and the program in Listing 4.2 demonstrates how the error handler can be installed in the parser to detect and report errors. The application does nothing more than read an XML document and check for errors. The parser always determines whether an XML document is well-formed, and this application can optionally be instructed to make certain that the document is also valid according to the definitions in its DTD. You can think of these simple classes as a kind of "hello world" program for the SAX API.

MyErrorHandler

SAX parse errors are handle by an `ErrorHandler` object that is registered with the parser; that is, a SAX error handler is a class that implements the `org.xml .sax.ErrorHandler` interface. This interface defines three methods. A method is to Java what a function is to C and a procedure is Ada. Whenever there is an error of any kind, one of the callback methods defined in the interface is called. Which method is called depends on the level, or severity, of the error message. It can be classed as a warning, an error, or a fatal error, which are defined as follows:

Warning. A warning indicates that something is out of the ordinary, but it does not prevent parsing from continuing. The parser doesn't think it has lost track of where it is in the source document. In your error handler, if you prefer, you can report warnings and then continue by returning from the callback method instead of throwing an exception

Error. An error is something that is wrong with the document (such as an unknown element), but the fundamentals of the parsing action are still intact enough for the parser to continue. Something will be missing or misshapen in the final output because the parser had to skip something it didn't recognize, but it is still possible for the parser output to be usable data. You must decide whether you want to try to continue to process the data from the parser and recover what you can from the unparsed remains of the input document by simply reporting the error and returning from the callback method or to throw an exception that will halt the parse.

Fatal error. A fatal error occurs when something about the document is not well-formed, and the parser would probably be lost if it were to continue. In fact, once a fatal error has been reported, it is no longer required that the parser be in a mode where it is possible to continue or even to report any further errors it may find if it does continue. The best thing to do in this callback method is to report the error and throw a SAXException to halt the parsing process.

Listing 4.1 demonstrates the implementation of a simple error handler.

```java
import org.xml.sax.SAXException;
import org.xml.sax.SAXParseException;
import org.xml.sax.ErrorHandler;

public class MyErrorHandler implements ErrorHandler {
    public void warning(SAXParseException e) throws SAXException {
        show("Warning",e);
        throw(e);
    }
    public void error(SAXParseException e) throws SAXException {
        show("Error",e);
        throw(e);
    }
    public void fatalError(SAXParseException e) throws SAXException {
        show("Fatal Error",e);
        throw(e);
    }
    private void show(String type,SAXParseException e) {
        System.out.println(type + ": " + e.getMessage());
        System.out.println("Line " + e.getLineNumber() +
                " Column " + e.getColumnNumber());
        System.out.println("System ID: " + e.getSystemId());
    }
}
```

Listing 4.1   A Simple Implementation of the ErrorHandler Interface

The show() method of MyErrorHandler in Listing 4.1 is used to format the error message from the data found in the SAXParseException passed to it. The following is an example of the output for a fatal error message. It indicates that on line 7 of TextDoc3.xml there is an element that is missing its closing tag:

```
Fatal Error: Expected "</name>" to terminate element starting on line 7.
Line 7 Column -1
System ID: file:/home/doc/book/jx/04/code/TestDoc3.xml
```

The value of the line number (Line 7) is dependable, but as you can see from this example, the parser may fail to report the correct column number. (In this example, Column -1 is used to indicate that the exact column number was not available when the SAXParseException was being created).

The interface defines three error callback methods, one representing each of the three levels of error conditions. In all three cases a SAXParseException (which is a SAXException) is passed to the callback method. This sample program ignores the level indication and treats all three the same way; it displays information about the error and then throws an exception that halts the parse.

SAXCheck

The SAXCheck class of Listing 4.2 is the mainline of a program that uses SAX to parse an XML document and report any error that it finds. It accepts the name of the XML document as an argument on the command line. It then creates a SAX parser with an error handler and parses the document. It ignores any incoming data that is produced as a result of the parse; it only runs the parser to check for errors. The error handler it uses is the MyErrorHandler shown in Listing 4.1.

In Listing 4.2 the XMLReader method setErrorHandler() is called to assign a MyErrorHandler object as the parser's error handler. If the error handler receives a callback, it reports it and throws an exception that is not caught in this program. The result is that whenever this program produces no output, the XML document is well-formed and valid. If, on the other hand, an error or warning is encountered, it is reported and the program stops.

SAXParserFactory

An object of the SAXParserFactory class is used in SAXCheck to create an actual SAX parser. The factory class contains a static method named newInstance() that is called to create an instance of itself; its constructor is protected, so this method is the only way to get a copy. It is done this way to make it possible for the parser factory to come from another source. That is, if you are in a situation where a number of different SAX parsers can be made available, an instance of the SAXParserFactory can be made to select from among them and return the appropriate one from the call to newInstance(). In the current version of JAXP there is only one SAX parser. The following are the steps the newInstance() method follows to find the class name of a SAXParserFactory to create the requested factory:

```java
import javax.xml.parsers.SAXParser;
import javax.xml.parsers.SAXParserFactory;
import org.xml.sax.InputSource;
import org.xml.sax.XMLReader;
import org.xml.sax.SAXException;
import java.io.*;

public class SAXCheck {
    static public void main(String[] arg) {
        String filename = null;
        boolean validate = false;

        if(arg.length == 1) {
            filename = arg[0];
        } else if(arg.length == 2) {
            if(!arg[0].equals("-v"))
                usage();
            validate = true;
            filename = arg[1];
        } else {
            usage();
        }

        // Create a new factory to create parsers that will
        // validate or not, according to the flag setting.
        SAXParserFactory spf = SAXParserFactory.newInstance();
        spf.setValidating(validate);

        // Create the XMLReader to be used to check for errors.
        XMLReader reader = null;
        try {
            SAXParser parser = spf.newSAXParser();
            reader = parser.getXMLReader();
        } catch (Exception e) {
            System.err.println(e);
            System.exit(1);
        }

        // Install an error handler in the reader.
        reader.setErrorHandler(new MyErrorHandler());

        // Use the XMLReader to parse the entire file.
        try {
            InputSource is = new InputSource(filename);
            reader.parse(is);
        } catch (SAXException e) {
            System.exit(1);
        } catch (IOException e) {
            System.err.println(e);
            System.exit(1);
        }
    }
    private static void usage() {
        System.err.println("Usage: SAXCheck [-v] <filename>");
        System.exit(1);
    }
}
```

Listing 4.2 Installation and Use of an Error Handler in a SAX Parser

1. If the system property javax.xml.SAXParserFactory is set, its value is used as the name of the class. This property can be stored as a persistent system property and used that way. Also, this property can be set from inside your program, so this is a technique by which you could select from among a group of available parser factories. See java.util.Properties in the Java API documentation that is a part of your Java installation.

2. If a file named lib/jaxp.properties exists, it is read by the newInstance() method. This file is in the standard Java properties format (see java.util .Properties in the Java API documentation). If the file contains a definition for the property java.xml.SAXParserFactory, its value is used. This is also a technique you could use to select from among your own group of parser factories.

3. If the JAR Services API is available, the available jar files will be searched for the class META-INF/services/javax.xml.parsers.SAXParserFactory.

4. The default SAXParserFactory of the JAXP is used.

If any one of these steps encounters an error, or if the default factory cannot be created, a FactoryConfigurationError is thrown.

Parsers always check to see if a document is well-formed because, if is not, it cannot be parsed. However, the method setValidating() can be used to specify whether manufactured parsers should also validate the XML code they read. The default is false. There is also a method named setNamespaceAware() that accepts a boolean argument that specifies whether the parser is to have the ability of processing name-spaces. This default is also false.

There is a method named setFeature() that can be used to specify whether a specific feature is on or off. Each feature is specified by its URI name. For example, the following enables namespace processing to occur:

```
spf.setFeature("http://xml.org/sax/features/namespaces",true);
```

The name of a feature is in the form of a URI to guarantee uniqueness. It is important to name them this way because it is possible to create and configure different parser factories, each one having its own set of options; using a different URI for the name of each option prevents name collisions. The following is the short list of features that are defined for all parser factories, including the one supplied with the JAXP. The first two are the same options that are set and cleared by calling setValidating() and setNamespaceAware().

http://xml.org/sax/features/validation. If true, the parser also checks for document validity. If false, the parser only checks for the document being well-formed.

http://xml.org/sax/features/namespaces. If true, the parser performs namespace processing. If false, the colons are simply included as another character in the simple names.

http://xml.org/sax/features/namespace-prefixes. If true, the parser reports the original prefixed names and attributes. If false, neither attributes nor namespace declarations are reported.

http://xml.org/sax/features/string-interning. If true, all of the names, prefixes, attributes, and URIs are internalized by java.lang.String.intern(). (In Java, internalizing prevents duplication of identical strings in internal storage.) If false, the strings may or may not be internalized, depending on the JVM.

http://xml.org/sax/features/external-general-entities. If true, all external text entities are included. If false, they are not included.

http://xml.org/sax/features/external-parameter-entities. If true, all external parameter entities, as well as the external DTD subset, are included. If false, they are not included.

XMLReader

As shown in Listing 4.2, there are two actions necessary to create an XMLReader. The first step is to get a SAXParser from the SAXParserFactory. The second step is to treat the SAXParser like a factory and get a SAXReader object from it. This two-step procedure is necessary because programs that use the SAX1 API must be compatible with those using SAX2. A SAX1 program will use the methods in the SAXParser to read and parse the XML, whereas a SAX2 program is capable of using the methods of the SAXReader to do the same thing. Unlike SAX1, SAX2, with the SAXReader, has additional capabilities and options made available to the program (such as namespaces and entity processing).

The XMLReader interface is implemented by a SAX parser. In other words, when you retrieve the XMLReader, you are actually retrieving a copy of the parser. It is used to parse XML, but the interface also defines methods for setting and querying features. It has a setFeature() method that works the same way, and has the same options available, as the setFeature() method of the SAXParserFactory.

With the XMLReader in Listing 4.2 the method setErrorHandler() is used to specify the object that is to be responsible for fielding any errors found during the parse of the XML. If you don't specify an error handler, the parse might silently fail and you would never know it (unless, of course, you tried to use the data that resulted from the parse).

The XMLReader interface defines two parse() methods. The one used in the example accepts an org.xml.xax.InputSource object as the input source. The other parse() method accepts the URI of the XML source file to be parsed. For example, to parse a file located on a Web site, you could use the following form:

```
reader.parse("http://fredtheurl/TextDoc3.xml");
```

Both of the parse() methods are blocking. That is, they do not return until the parse has been completed.

SAX Document Lister

In the program shown in Listing 4.3, the SAX parser is used to parse an XML document, and then the result of the parse is displayed as each piece of the document is passed to the application. The basic structure of this sample program is very much like

```
import javax.xml.parsers.SAXParser;
import javax.xml.parsers.SAXParserFactory;
import org.xml.sax.InputSource;
import org.xml.sax.XMLReader;
import org.xml.sax.SAXException;
import java.io.*;

public class SAXDump {
    static public void main(String[] arg) {
        String filename = null;

        if(arg.length == 1) {
            filename = arg[0];
        } else {
            usage();
        }

        // Create a new factory that will create the parser.
        SAXParserFactory spf = SAXParserFactory.newInstance();

        // Create the XMLReader to be used to parse the document.
        XMLReader reader = null;
        try {
            SAXParser parser = spf.newSAXParser();
            reader = parser.getXMLReader();
        } catch (Exception e) {
            System.err.println(e);
            System.exit(1);
        }

        // Specify the error handler and the content handler.
        reader.setErrorHandler(new MyErrorHandler());
        reader.setContentHandler(new MyContentHandler());

        // Use the XMLReader to parse the entire file.
        try {
            InputSource is = new InputSource(filename);
            reader.parse(is);
        } catch (SAXException e) {
            System.exit(1);
        } catch (IOException e) {
            System.err.println(e);
            System.exit(1);
        }
    }
    private static void usage() {
        System.err.println("Usage: SAXDump <filename>");
        System.exit(1);
    }
}
```

Listing 4.3   A Program to Display the Input from a SAX Parser

the one in Listing 4.2. Both programs use the same error handler. The only real difference between the two is that, with SAXDump in Listing 4.3, a ContentHandler is added to receive and respond to the results of the parse.

MyContentHandler

In Listing 4.3 there is a call to the setContentHandler() method of the XMLReader to register a ContentHandler object that will assume the task of receiving the parsed information:

```
reader.setContentHandler(new MyContentHandler());
```

In this case the ContentHandler object is an instance of the MyContentHandler class shown in Listing 4.4. The parsed data is passed, piece by piece, to the process in the form of callback methods in the same manner as events are passed to event handlers. In fact, the SAX parsing process is often referred to as *event handling*.

The MyContentHandler class in Listing 4.4 implements the interface org.xml .sax.ContentHandler. The interface defines 11 methods that are to be called to pass the data from the parser to the application. Each one of these methods, described individually in the next section, receives one specific type of information extracted from the XML document by the parser. The data from the XML document is not organized or rearranged in any way by the parser; each piece of the input document is simply extracted and used as arguments to the appropriate method, and this is done by the parser as each piece is encountered.

A SAX application only has to implement the methods of the ContentHandler interface and have each method process the arriving data according to its markup. The example in Listing 4.4 simply displays the information that arrives.

```
import org.xml.sax.ContentHandler;
import org.xml.sax.Attributes;
import org.xml.sax.Locator;

public class MyContentHandler implements ContentHandler {
    private Locator locator;
    /** The name and of the SAX document and the current
        location within the document. */
    public void setDocumentLocator(Locator locator) {
        this.locator = locator;
        System.out.println("-" + locator.getLineNumber() +
            "---Document ID: " +  locator.getSystemId());
    }

    /** The parsing of a document has started.. */
    public void startDocument() {
```

Listing 4.4   A Program to Run a SAX Parser and Display the Parse Data   (*continues*)

```
        System.out.println("-" + locator.getLineNumber() +
            "---Document parse started");
    }

    /** The parsing of a document has completed.. */
    public void endDocument() {
        System.out.println("-" + locator.getLineNumber() +
            "---Document parse ended");
    }

    /** The start of a namespace scope */
    public void startPrefixMapping(String prefix,String uri) {
        System.out.println("-" + locator.getLineNumber() +
            "---Namespace scope begins");
        System.out.println("      " + prefix + "=\"" + uri + "\"");
    }

    /** The end of a namespace scope */
    public void endPrefixMapping(String prefix)  {
        System.out.println("-" + locator.getLineNumber() +
            "---Namespace scope ends");
        System.out.println("      " + prefix);
    }

    /** The opening tag of an element.*/
    public void startElement(String namespaceURI,String localName,
            String qName,Attributes atts) {
        System.out.println("-" + locator.getLineNumber() +
            "---Opening tag of an element");
        System.out.println("       Namespace: " + namespaceURI);
        System.out.println("      Local name: " + localName);
        System.out.println("  Qualified name: " + qName);
        for(int i=0; i<atts.getLength(); i++) {
            System.out.println("        Attribute: " + atts.getQName(i) +
                "=\"" + atts.getValue(i) + "\"");
        }
    }

    /** The closing tag of an element. */
    public void endElement(String namespaceURI,String localName,
            String qName) {
        System.out.println("-" + locator.getLineNumber() +
            "---Closing tag of an element");
        System.out.println("       Namespace: " + namespaceURI);
        System.out.println("      Local name: " + localName);
        System.out.println("  Qualified name: " + qName);
    }

    /** Character data. */
    public void characters(char[] ch,int start,int length) {
```

Listing 4.4   *(continues)*

```
        System.out.println("-" + locator.getLineNumber() +
            "---Character data");
        showCharacters(ch,start,length);
    }

    /** Ignorable whitespace character data. */
    public void ignorableWhitespace(char[] ch,int start,int length) {
        System.out.println("-" + locator.getLineNumber() +
            "---Whitespace");
        showCharacters(ch,start,length);
    }

    /** Processing Instruction */
    public void processingInstruction(String target,String data) {
        System.out.println("-" + locator.getLineNumber() +
            "---Processing Instruction");
        System.out.println("          Target: " + target);
        System.out.println("            Data: " + data);
    }

    /** A skipped entity.*/
    public void skippedEntity(String name) {
        System.out.println("-" + locator.getLineNumber() +
            "---Skipped Entity");
        System.out.println("            Name: " + name);
    }

    /** Internal method to format arrays of characters so the
        special whitespace characters will show. */
    public void showCharacters(char[] ch,int start,int length) {
        System.out.print("         \"");
        for(int i=start; i<start + length; i++)
            switch(ch[i]) {
            case '\n':
                System.out.print("\\n");
                break;
            case '\r':
                System.out.print("\\r");
                break;
            case '\t':
                System.out.print("\\t");
                break;
            default:
                System.out.print(ch[i]);
                break;
            }
        System.out.println("\"");
    }
}
```

Listing 4.4   *(continued)*

As the parser proceeds through the text of the XML document, it will call the callback method that is appropriate for whatever it finds. An application simply implements the callback methods so that they will do whatever they should do when a certain element, block of text, processing instruction (PI), or some other part of XML, is encountered by the parser.

The `ContentHandler` Callback Methods

The `ContentHandler` interface defines a set of callback methods used by a SAX parser to pass data into an application. Each of these methods is responsible for handling one particular type of data. The following list describes the XML input that causes each callback method to be called and what is passed to the method:

`setDocumentLocator()` This method is called just as the parser gets itself set up ready to start reading the XML document. The SAX specification does not strictly require that this method be called but, if it is, it is the first one to be called. The `Locator` object contains the name of the document being parsed along with a running line number, which can be used by an application for status messages.

`startDocument()` This method is called just to notify the application that the parsing has begun. It is always called at the very beginning of the parse, after `setDocumentLocator()` but before any of the methods that supply data.

`endDocument()` This method is called at the very end to notify the application that parsing is complete and no more data will be arriving.

`startPrefixMapping()` This method is called whenever there is an internal namespace name being associated with its URI. In most cases this information is not necessary because the other methods—the ones that are called with the tag names—always include the namespace prefix and its URI along with the name of the tag. However, this method is called because there could be a situation where namespace scoping needs to be tracked. A call to this method will mark the point at which the namespace is first declared.

`endPrefixMapping()` This method is called when exiting the scope of a previously declared start of a prefix mapping. For each call to `startPrefixMapping()` there is a matching call to `endPrefixMapping()`. The calls that start and end prefix mapping do not necessarily occur in properly nested order. For example, if three calls to `startPrefixMapping()` open the scope of aa, bb, and cc, it is possible that the call to `endPrefixMapping()` would close their scopes in some other order, such as bb, cc, and aa.

`startElement()` This method is called for each opening tag. The arguments passed to the method include the name of the tag and all of its attributes. The namespace is included in the form of its URI, which means that it is possible for an application to process an XML document and completely ignore the internal names it uses for the namespaces; the URI names can be used to guarantee identity of the appropriate namespace. The list of attributes includes only the attributes that were explicitly specified; that is, `#IMPLIED` attributes are not included.

`endElement()` This method is called for each closing tag. There is a matching call to `endElement()` for each call to `startElement()`. Any data contained in the element will have already been passed to the application; that is, proper nesting of tags is maintained. This method is called even when the element is empty.

characters() This method is called with any text found inside an element. It normally comes as a single block of text, but it is possible that multiple calls to characters() may be executed to deliver large blocks of text in pieces. The string is passed in as an array of characters with two integers that specify the index to the first character and a count of the number of characters. For example, if the characters in the array are a, b, c, d, e, and f, and the two integer values are 2 and 4, the only characters being passed in are c, d, and e. Characters in the array outside of those specified as being part of string should be considered off limits to the callback method. Some character arrays may also be sent to the application with a call to ignorableWhitespace() instead of a call to characters().

ignorableWhitespace() This method is called with whitespace strings. If the parser is not validating, there is no way it can determine whether any particular string of whitespace can be ignored, so it will probably send all of the strings to the application by calling characters(). If the parser is validating, and it discovers a string of whitespace that is not defined in the DTD, it is required to call this method with the whitespace string. That means, for a validating parser, only validated strings are passed to characters().

processingInstruction() This method is called for each PI. Recall that the content of a PI is a name followed by some free-form text. The parser breaks up the content of the PI into two strings—all characters up to the first space are assumed to be the name—and passes each of the two pieces, otherwise intact, to the callback method.

skippedEntity() This method may be called by some parsers when they encounter an entity that is not defined. Say, for example, a parser is not set to do validating and it encounters the use of an entity that is defined in a remote DTD. The parser will not know what to do with it, so it can choose to call the skippedEntity() method.

Executing the SAX Parser

The program named SAXDump in Listing 4.3 uses a SAX parser to read XML and uses the ContentHandler shown in Listing 4.4 to receive the data from the parse. The XML document shown in Listing 4.5 is used as input to produce the text of Listing 4.6.

In MyContentHandler, each of the callback methods prints a brief description indicating which method has been called. This description includes the current line number, which is retrieved from the Locator object that was provided to the setDocumentLocater() callback method. The resulting output from using Listing 4.5 as input looks like that shown in Listing 4.6.

Because this was not a validating parse—which means there was no DTD involved—the parser had no way of knowing which strings of characters can be ignored. Notice that the character data reported to be on line 3 consists of one newline and one tab character:

```
<?xml version="1.0" standalone="yes"?>
<contacts:folks xmlns:contacts="fredtheurl/contacts">
    <?winsize height="22" width="40"?>
    <contacts:person>
        <contacts:name>Bertha D. Blues</contacts:name>
        <contacts:phone type="home">907 555-8901</contacts:phone>
        <contacts:email>bertha@homernet.net;</contacts:email>
    </contacts:person>
</contacts:folks>
```

Listing 4.5   An XML Document

```
-3---Character data
        "\n\t"
```

These characters are simply the end of a line (newline) and the indention at the beginning of the next line (tab). If the parser had been able to look into a DTD to determine that
no text belonged there, it could have discarded it by calling ignorableWhitespace()
instead of characters(). As you look through the example output, you will see several character lines, such as the ones on lines 4 and 5, that consist of a newline character followed by tabs or spaces. These all are the indentions that were placed in the XML
to make it more readable to humans. This is the whitespace dilemma faced by the
parsers and shows why the treatment of whitespace in XML is considered inconsistent.
It really isn't inconsistent, but you do need to know how to work with it.

Notice that both the opening tag and closing tag of an element supply the tag name
in three different forms:

```
Namespace: fredtheurl/contacts
     Local name: folks
  Qualified name: contacts:folks
```

The local name is the simple name of the tag with the namespace information omitted.
The qualified name is the tag name exactly as it appears in the XML document. The
namespace name is the URI associated with the namespace. If, in your application, you
only refer to the URI and the local name, there is no need to ever be concerned with the
name used inside the XML. This means that several different people can write documents based on the same DTD and use whatever internal namespace name they would
like; if your program can process one of these documents, it can process them all.

SAX calls the methods sequentially no matter what it encounters. It doesn't join split
pieces back together. For example, a modification could be made to the XML document
in Listing 4.5 to include a nested tag:

```
<contacts:name>Bertha <bold>D.</bold> Blues</contacts:name>
```

The printed output from running the program would look like the following, which
demonstrates that the form of the output is unchanged from the original shown in
Listing 4.6 except that the new nested tag has been inserted:

```
-5---Opening tag of an element
        Namespace: fredtheurl/contacts
        Local name: name
   Qualified name: contacts:name
-5---Character data
        "Bertha "
-5---Opening tag of an element
        Namespace:
        Local name: bold
   Qualified name: bold
-5---Character data
        "D."
-5---Closing tag of an element
        Namespace:
        Local name: bold
   Qualified name: bold
-5---Character data
        " Blues"
-5---Closing tag of an element
        Namespace: fredtheurl/contacts
        Local name: name
   Qualified name: contacts:name
```

```
-1---Document ID: file:/home/doc/book/jx/04/code/TestDoc4.xml
-1---Document parse started
-2---Namespace scope begins
     contacts="fredtheurl/contacts"
-2---Opening tag of an element
        Namespace: fredtheurl/contacts
        Local name: folks
   Qualified name: contacts:folks
-3---Character data
        "\n\t"
-3---Processing Instruction
        Target: winsize
          Data: height="22" width="40"
-4---Character data
        "\n    "
-4---Opening tag of an element
        Namespace: fredtheurl/contacts
        Local name: person
   Qualified name: contacts:person
-5---Character data
        "\n       "
-5---Opening tag of an element
        Namespace: fredtheurl/contacts
        Local name: name
```

Listing 4.6   Example Output from `MyContentHandler`   (continues)

```
   Qualified name: contacts:name
-5---Character data
        "Bertha D. Blues"
-5---Closing tag of an element
        Namespace: fredtheurl/contacts
        Local name: name
   Qualified name: contacts:name
-6---Character data
        "\n          "
-6---Opening tag of an element
        Namespace: fredtheurl/contacts
        Local name: phone
   Qualified name: contacts:phone
        Attribute: type="home"
-6---Character data
        "907 555-8901"
-6---Closing tag of an element
        Namespace: fredtheurl/contacts
        Local name: phone
   Qualified name: contacts:phone
-7---Character data
        "\n          "
-7---Opening tag of an element
        Namespace: fredtheurl/contacts
        Local name: email
   Qualified name: contacts:email
-7---Character data
        "bertha@homernet.net;"
-7---Closing tag of an element
        Namespace: fredtheurl/contacts
        Local name: email
   Qualified name: contacts:email
-8---Character data
        "\n     "
-8---Closing tag of an element
        Namespace: fredtheurl/contacts
        Local name: person
   Qualified name: contacts:person
-9---Character data
        "\n"
-9---Closing tag of an element
        Namespace: fredtheurl/contacts
        Local name: folks
   Qualified name: contacts:folks
-9---Namespace scope ends
     contacts
-10---Document parse ended
```

Listing 4.6   *(continued)*

Notice a couple of important distinctions: First, each piece of the string separated by the nested tag is treated as a completely separate item. Second, the element name `bold` does not have a namespace, so the namespace provided to the callback method is a zero-length string, and the local name is the same as the qualified name.

Summary

The SAX parser can be used in your application with very little programming effort. The classes presented in this chapter are complete in all respects except for the application code that you will use to interpret the input for processing into whatever form of output you would like. As shown in this chapter, it is quite straightforward to create a detailed ASCII listing of selected information from an XML document. The same process can be used to output the data as HTML, or some other graphic format, to display it. The job of the SAX parser is to supply your program with the information from an XML document in such a way that you can easily get to it and do whatever you like with it. And that is the subject of the next chapter. Chapter 5 contains examples of programs that read XML documents and output the content in a different form.

CHAPTER

5

SAX Document Manipulation

SAX reads through an XML document sequentially and passes the information to your program in the same order it finds it. This procedure is sufficient for you to write a program that manually translates the XML input into some other form. This chapter contains some basic examples and explanations of using SAX to read an XML document and translate the output into some other form.

Although there are some very useful things you can do using the SAX parser, there are some limitations. If you need to keep track of things, or change the order of things, you will have to write code to do that yourself. For example, if there is a list of items in the document, and you need to know how many there are before you can process them, you will have to store the entire list in your program as you count them and then process them from the stored list. SAX is a simple parser with simple output into your program, and sometimes all you need is something to do a simple job.

The type of things you can do using only SAX generally involve making simple changes such as removing data, adding data, or converting the input document to another form that is not laid out too differently from the original. An advantage of the SAX parser is that it is so simple that implementing relatively simple chores is easy. This chapter demonstrates how to write programs that do simple chores.

Duplicate a Document

The process of duplicating a document is fairly straightforward because the document arrives from the SAX parser in the same order it appeared in the original document. There are a couple of special situations that must be handled but, for the most part, it is simply a matter of formatting the input from the parser into an output file.

The program shown in Listing 5.1 uses the two arguments supplied on the command line as the names of the input and output files. The first argument is the name of the input XML file and the second is the name of an output file. Very much like the examples presented in Chapter 4, this program uses a SAXParserFactory to create a SAXParser to read the input. The same class developed in Chapter 4, the one named MyErrorHandler, is set as the error handler for the parser.

The program in Listing 5.1 uses the second argument as the name of a new XML file that will receive the output text. The file is opened for output as a PrintWriter object, and this object is passed to the constructor of a class named MyCopyHandler. As shown in Listing 5.2, the MyCopyHandler class implements the ContentHandler interface, so it will be capable of receiving a method call for each of the XML items the parser encounters in the input file. This class is very similar to the classes in the previous chapter that simply dump the results coming from the parser, but the output from this one is a bit different because it is formatted as XML.

After the parser makes its initial call to setDocumentLocator(), the next method called in Listing 5.2 is startDocument(). Every XML document must begin with a declaration line, and because the declaration information is not passed through the SAX parser, it is necessary to create one and write it to the output.

When writing the output XML, there is no need to specify end of lines or spacing because that is retained, in its entirety, from the input and copied to the output through the method characters() and ignorableWhitespace(). If these two methods simply echo to the output everything that comes to them from the input, the format of the output will be exactly the same as the input. This means the method named startElement() can just write the tag information to the output without worrying about position.

The method startElement() is called whenever a new opening tag is encountered. There are two things that could be a part of the element. It could contain a namespace declaration, and it could contain one or more attribute settings. Handling the attributes is straightforward; the method simply loops through them and copies the name and its value (in the correct format) to the output file. The namespace declaration is a bit different. If there is a namespace declaration in the element, the element takes on the following basic form:

```
<spacename:tagname xmlns:spacename="http://some/uri">
```

This is the one point at which SAX breaks with its own tradition and does things out of order, or at least seems to. The method startPrefixMapping() is called before the call to startElement(). This sequence has the advantage that the namespace definition is announced before the call to startElement(), which seems to use the namespace name before it is actually defined. This order can be important if you have a process that is tracking namespaces because, if the portion of a name in front of the

```java
import javax.xml.parsers.SAXParser;
import javax.xml.parsers.SAXParserFactory;
import javax.xml.parsers.ParserConfigurationException;
import org.xml.sax.InputSource;
import org.xml.sax.XMLReader;
import org.xml.sax.SAXException;
import java.io.*;

public class SAXCopy {
    static public void main(String[] arg) {
        String infilename = null;
        String outfilename = null;
        if(arg.length == 2) {
            infilename = arg[0];
            outfilename = arg[1];
        } else {
            usage();
        }

        try {
            SAXParserFactory spf = SAXParserFactory.newInstance();
            SAXParser parser = spf.newSAXParser();
            XMLReader reader = parser.getXMLReader();
            reader.setErrorHandler(new MyErrorHandler());
            FileOutputStream fos = new FileOutputStream(outfilename);
            PrintWriter out = new PrintWriter(fos);
            MyCopyHandler duper = new MyCopyHandler(out);
            reader.setContentHandler(duper);
            InputSource is = new InputSource(infilename);
            reader.parse(is);
            out.close();
        } catch (SAXException e) {
            System.exit(1);
        } catch (ParserConfigurationException e) {
            System.err.println(e);
            System.exit(1);
        } catch (IOException e) {
            System.err.println(e);
            System.exit(1);
        }
    }
    private static void usage() {
        System.err.println("Usage: SAXCopy <infile> <outfile>");
        System.exit(1);
    }
}
```

Listing 5.1   The Mainline of an Application That Duplicates XML Files

```java
import org.xml.sax.ContentHandler;
import org.xml.sax.Attributes;
import org.xml.sax.Locator;
import java.io.*;

public class MyCopyHandler implements ContentHandler {
    private boolean namespaceBegin = false;
    private String currentNamespace;
    private String currentNamespaceUri;
    private Locator locator;
    private PrintWriter out;
    public MyCopyHandler(PrintWriter out) {
        this.out = out;
    }
    public void setDocumentLocator(Locator locator) {
        this.locator = locator;
    }

    public void startDocument() {
        out.println("<?xml version=\"1.0\"?>");
        out.println();
    }

    public void endDocument() {
    }

    public void startPrefixMapping(String prefix,String uri) {
        namespaceBegin = true;
        currentNamespace = prefix;
        currentNamespaceUri = uri;
    }

    public void endPrefixMapping(String prefix)  {
    }

    public void startElement(String namespaceURI,String localName,
            String qName,Attributes atts) {
        out.print("<" + qName);
        if(namespaceBegin) {
            out.print(" xmlns:" + currentNamespace + "=\"" +
                    currentNamespaceUri + "\"");
            namespaceBegin = false;
        }
        for(int i=0; i<atts.getLength(); i++) {
            out.print(" " + atts.getQName(i) + "=\\" +
                    atts.getValue(i) + "\"");
        }
        out.print(">");
    }
```

Listing 5.2 A Class to Convert SAX Parse Information into an XML Document

(continues)

```
    public void endElement(String namespaceURI,String localName,
            String qName) {
        out.print("</" + qName + ">");
    }

    public void characters(char[] ch,int start,int length) {
        for(int i=start; i<start + length; i++)
            out.print(ch[i]);
    }

    public void ignorableWhitespace(char[] ch,int start,int length) {
        for(int i=start; i<start + length; i++)
            out.print(ch[i]);
    }

    public void processingInstruction(String target,String data) {
        out.print("<?" + target + " " + data + "?>");
    }

    public void skippedEntity(String name) {
        out.print("&" + name + ";");
    }
}
```

Listing 5.2   *(continued)*

colon is not a namespace, it is assumed to be simply a part of the tag name. All of this means that the program that duplicates the XML must store the namespace definition for output in the proper order. Notice that the method startPrefixMapping() stores the information and sets the flag named namespaceBegin. Then, in startElement(), if namespaceBegin has been set to true, the xmlns definition is written to the output.

One part of the output from this program may be written differently from the input: It is possible for an element to be defined in the input as a single tag by using a terminator character. Such a tag would appear as follows:

```
<somename mattr="value"/>
```

Because the parser makes two method calls, one to startElement() and one to endElement(), for this one tag, and because the program does not bother to track whether there has been an intervening body to the element, the output will default to the following form:

```
<somename mattr="value"></somename>
```

The two mean exactly the same thing, so there is no real problem. The program could be modified to detect this condition by checking to see if any other method was called between the opening and closing tags.

Extracting XML Text

If you need to, you can easily extract data from an XML document by checking the tag names and extracting the data as each element is passed to the methods of the content handler. The example shown in Listing 5.5 is a content handler that accepts input from an XML document containing a list of names, numbers, and email addresses. An example of an XML document in the correct format is shown in Listing 5.3. Notice that inside the person elements, the order of the name, number, and email elements do vary. In fact, there are a couple of person elements that contain incomplete entries. Incomplete data records are handled by the program that extracts the data and outputs it in a different form; the output is shown in Listing 5.4, where the names are listed, in alphabetical order, in a simple text file.

```xml
<?xml version="1.0" standalone="yes"?>

<folks>
    <person>
        <phone>907 555-8901</phone>
        <email>lifar@homernet.net</email>
        <name>Riley, Lifa</name>
    </person>
    <person>
        <phone>314 555-9910</phone>
        <name>Valee, Rudy</name>
        <email>rv@belugalake.com</email>
    </person>
    <person>
        <name>Blues, Bertha D.</name>
        <email>bertha@xyz.net</email>
    </person>
    <person>
        <name>Cugat, Xavier</name>
        <email>cugie@nosuch.net</email>
    </person>
    <person>
        <phone>502 555-2192</phone>
        <name>Baker, Mary</name>
    </person>
    <person>
        <phone>314 555-7092</phone>
        <email>holly@xyz.net</email>
        <name>Lane, Holly</name>
    </person>
</folks>
```

Listing 5.3   An XML Document Containing a Simple Contact List

```
   name                     phone                   email
   ----                     -----                   ------
Baker, Mary              502 555-2192            none
Blues, Bertha D.         none                    bertha@xyz.net
Cugat, Xavier            none                    cugie@nosuch.net
Lane,  Holly             314 555-7092            holly@xyz.net
Riley, Lifa              907 555-8901            lifar@homernet.net
Valee, Rudy              314 555-9910            rv@belugalake.com
```

Listing 5.4   Data Extracted from an XML Document and Formatted as Text

To create a program that will translate the XML in Listing 5.3 into the table in Listing 5.4, there is no need to write an entire new program. All that is necessary is to write a new content handler like the one shown in Listing 5.5. The mainline of the program is almost identical to the one in Listing 5.1. There is only one minor change that needs to be made to tell the program to use a different content handler. Remove the following line, which is the one that creates the ContentHandler object:

```
MyCopyHandler duper = new MyCopyHandler(out);
```

In its place insert a new line that will create a different ContentHandler to format the data according to the tags:

```
MyTextHandler duper = new MyTextHandler(out);
```

```
import org.xml.sax.ContentHandler;
import org.xml.sax.Attributes;
import org.xml.sax.Locator;
import java.util.Vector;
import java.io.*;

public class MyTextHandler implements ContentHandler {
    private boolean insideNameElement = false;
    private boolean insidePhoneElement = false;
    private boolean insideEmailElement = false;
    private Person person;
    private Vector personVec;
    private PrintWriter out;
    public MyTextHandler(PrintWriter out) {
        this.out = out;
        personVec = new Vector();
    }
    public void setDocumentLocator(Locator locator) {
    }
```

Listing 5.5   A Content Handler to Output a Sorted List   (continues)

```
public void startDocument() {
    putCols(" name"," phone"," email");
    putCols(" ----"," -----"," -----");
}

public void endDocument() {
    int k1 = 1;
    while(k1 < personVec.size()) {
        int k0 = k1 - 1;
        Person p0 = (Person)personVec.elementAt(k0);
        Person p1 = (Person)personVec.elementAt(k1);
        if(p0.getName().compareTo(p1.getName()) > 0) {
            personVec.setElementAt(p0,k1);
            personVec.setElementAt(p1,k0);
            if(k1 > 1)
                k1--;
        } else {
            k1++;
        }
    }
    for(int i=0; i<personVec.size(); i++) {
        Person p = (Person)personVec.elementAt(i);
        putCols(p.getName(),p.getPhone(),p.getEmail());
    }
}

public void startPrefixMapping(String prefix,String uri) { }

public void endPrefixMapping(String prefix) { }

public void startElement(String namespaceURI,String localName,
        String qName,Attributes atts) {
    if(localName.equals("person")) {
        person = new Person();
    } else if(localName.equals("name")) {
        insideNameElement = true;
    } else if(localName.equals("phone")) {
        insidePhoneElement = true;
    } else if(localName.equals("email")) {
        insideEmailElement = true;
    }
}

public void endElement(String namespaceURI,String localName,
        String qName) {
    if(localName.equals("person")) {
        if(person != null)
            personVec.addElement(person);
    } else if(localName.equals("name")) {
        insideNameElement = false;
    } else if(localName.equals("phone")) {
```

Listing 5.5   (continues)

```
                     insidePhoneElement = false;
            } else if(localName.equals("email")) {
                insideEmailElement = false;
            }
        }

    public void characters(char[] ch,int start,int length) {
        String str = "";
        for(int i=start; i<start + length; i++)
            str += ch[i];
        if(insideNameElement)
            person.setName(str);
        else if(insidePhoneElement)
            person.setPhone(str);
        else if(insideEmailElement)
            person.setEmail(str);
    }

    public void ignorableWhitespace(char[] ch,int start,int length) { }

    public void processingInstruction(String target,String data) { }

    public void skippedEntity(String name) { }

    private void putCols(String col1,String col2,String col3) {
        String lout = col1;
        while(lout.length() < 25)
            lout += " ";
        lout += col2;
        while(lout.length() < 50)
            lout += " ";
        lout += col3;
        out.println(lout);
    }
}
```

Listing 5.5   (*continued*)

The new content handler, named `MyTextHandler`, is shown in Listing 5.5. It implements the methods of the `ContentHandler` interface, and these methods are called by the parser as it encounters items in the input XML document. Because of the linear nature of the input, the content handler must store the incoming data so that it can be output in sorted order. Flags must also be used to keep track of what type of element is currently being parsed so that, when text arrives, the content handler will know whether it is a name, a phone number, or an email address.

The content handler in Listing 5.5 does not have bodies defined to implement all of the methods required by the `ContentHandler` interface. The `setDocumentLocator()` method does nothing because this process never needs to know a location in the input document; if the program were more sophisticated and detected errors, the location information would be very useful for reporting the errors. The startPrefixMapping() and endPrefixMapping() methods serve no purpose because there are no namespaces in the input document. If there were namespaces, it might be necessary to keep track of which namespaces were active to help sort out element naming conflicts. There are also no bodies for ignorableWhitespace(), processingInstruction(), and skippedEntity() because there is no need to process such information.

The first method called is startDocument(), so it is used to output the column headings. Actually, in this case, there is no further output until the endDocument() method is called because all the data must be gathered and sorted; therefore, the column headings could just as well have been output there.

Whenever a new element is encountered in the input, the startElement() method is called with the element name. If it is a person element, a new Person object is created to hold the information from it. The Person class, shown in Listing 5.6, is a

```
public class Person {
    private String name = null;
    private String phone = null;
    private String email = null;
    public void setName(String value) {
        name = value;
    }
    public void setPhone(String value) {
        phone = value;
    }
    public void setEmail(String value) {
        email = value;
    }
    public String getName() {
        if(name == null)
            return("none");
        return(name);
    }
    public String getPhone() {
        if(phone == null)
            return("none");
        return(phone);
    }
    public String getEmail() {
        if(email == null)
            return("none");
        return(email);
    }
}
```

Listing 5.6   A Class for Holding Person Information

simple container for the name, phone, and email strings. If the element name in `startElement()` is a name, person, or email element, a flag is set to indicate that any incoming data was found inside that particular element type. The next method to be called, under normal circumstances, will be the `characters()` method with the actual content of the element. The type of data is determined in the `characters()` method by checking the flags, and the string is added to the current `Person` object. Next, the `endElement()` method is called, which allows the content handler to clear the flag that indicates the type of the current element; or if it is a `person` element, the current `Person` object has been filled with all the information available so that it is stored in the `Vector` object named `personVec` for future retrieval. All of this flag setting and clearing is necessary because the SAX parser has no context; it does not keep track of anything, so the program must do it.

The `Person` class in Listing 5.6 is capable of containing the three strings and returning them on request, or returning the string "none" if the requested string is not present. A collection of `Person` objects is stored in a `Vector` object. The `endDocument()` method of `MyTextHandler` uses a simple swap sort to alphabetize the names.

Formatting XML Text as HTML

The text of an XML document can be extracted and formatted into an HTML document by using the SAX parser. In fact, this was the original purpose for XML, and SAX is a clean and simple approach for doing so.

The process of creating HTML is the same as for creating any other text files. It is a matter of using a content handler to read the data extracted from the XML elements and then formatting the data into HTML. A content handler named `MyHtmlHandler` that creates HTML is shown in Listing 5.7. This content handler is the same as the one shown in Listing 5.5, which formats the data into a text file; the only difference is in the details of the output text.

```
import org.xml.sax.ContentHandler;
import org.xml.sax.Attributes;
import org.xml.sax.Locator;
import java.util.Vector;
import java.io.*;

public class MyHtmlHandler implements ContentHandler {
    private boolean insideNameElement = false;
    private boolean insidePhoneElement = false;
    private boolean insideEmailElement = false;
    private Person person;
    private Vector personVec;
    private PrintWriter out;
    public MyHtmlHandler(PrintWriter out) {
        this.out = out;
```

Listing 5.7   A Content Handler to Output a Sorted List as HTML   *(continues)*

```
            personVec = new Vector();
}
public void setDocumentLocator(Locator locator) { }

public void startDocument() { }

public void endDocument() {
    int k1 = 1;
    while(k1 < personVec.size()) {
        int k0 = k1 - 1;
        Person p0 = (Person)personVec.elementAt(k0);
        Person p1 = (Person)personVec.elementAt(k1);
        if(p0.getName().compareTo(p1.getName()) > 0) {
            personVec.setElementAt(p0,k1);
            personVec.setElementAt(p1,k0);
            if(k1 > 1)
                k1--;
        } else {
            k1++;
        }
    }

    out.println("<html>");
    out.println("<head>");
    out.println("  <title>Persons</title>");
    out.println("</head>");
    out.println("<body>");
    out.println("<center><h1>Persons</h1><center>");
    out.println("<hr>");

    out.println("<center>");
    out.println("<table border cellspacing=0 cellpadding=5>");
    out.println("  <caption align=top>");
    out.println("     A List of Names with Phone and Email");
    out.println("  </caption>");
    out.println("  <tr>");
    out.println("    <th>Name</th>");
    out.println("    <th>Phone</th>");
    out.println("    <th>Email</th>");
    out.println("  </tr>");

    for(int i=0; i<personVec.size(); i++) {
        Person p = (Person)personVec.elementAt(i);
        out.println("  <tr>");
        out.println("    <td>" + p.getName() + "</td>");
        out.println("    <td>" + p.getPhone() + "</td>");
        out.println("    <td>" + p.getEmail() + "</td>");
        out.println("  </tr>");
    }

    out.println("</table>");
    out.println("</center>");
    out.println("</body>");
    out.println("</html>");
```

Listing 5.7   *(continues)*

```
    }

    public void startPrefixMapping(String prefix,String uri) { }

    public void endPrefixMapping(String prefix)  { }

    public void startElement(String namespaceURI,String localName,
            String qName,Attributes atts) {
        if(localName.equals("person")) {
            person = new Person();
        } else if(localName.equals("name")) {
            insideNameElement = true;
        } else if(localName.equals("phone")) {
            insidePhoneElement = true;
        } else if(localName.equals("email")) {
            insideEmailElement = true;
        }
    }

    public void endElement(String namespaceURI,String localName,
            String qName) {
        if(localName.equals("person")) {
            if(person != null)
                personVec.addElement(person);
        } else if(localName.equals("name")) {
            insideNameElement = false;
        } else if(localName.equals("phone")) {
            insidePhoneElement = false;
        } else if(localName.equals("email")) {
            insideEmailElement = false;
        }
    }

    public void characters(char[] ch,int start,int length) {
        String str = "";
        for(int i=start; i<start + length; i++)
            str += ch[i];
        if(insideNameElement)
            person.setName(str);
        else if(insidePhoneElement)
            person.setPhone(str);
        else if(insideEmailElement)
            person.setEmail(str);
    }

    public void ignorableWhitespace(char[] ch,int start,int length) { }

    public void processingInstruction(String target,String data) { }

    public void skippedEntity(String name) { }
}
```

Listing 5.7   *(continued)*

```
<html>
<head>
  <title>Persons</title>
</head>
<body>
<center><h1>Persons</h1><center>
<hr>
<center>
<table border cellspacing=0 cellpadding=5>
  <caption align=top>
    A List of Names with Phone and Email
  </caption>
  <tr>
    <th>Name</th>
    <th>Phone</th>
    <th>Email</th>
  </tr>
  <tr>
    <td>Baker, Mary</td>
    <td>502 555-2192</td>
    <td>none</td>
  </tr>
  <tr>
    <td>Blues, Bertha D.</td>
    <td>none</td>
    <td>bertha@xyz.net</td>
  </tr>
  <tr>
    <td>Cugat, Xavier</td>
    <td>none</td>
    <td>cugie@nosuch.net</td>
  </tr>
  <tr>
    <td>Lane, Holly</td>
    <td>314 555-7092</td>
    <td>holly@xyz.net</td>
  </tr>
  <tr>
    <td>Riley, Lifa</td>
    <td>907 555-8901</td>
    <td>lifar@homernet.net</td>
  </tr>
  <tr>
    <td>Valee, Rudy</td>
    <td>314 555-9910</td>
    <td>rv@belugalake.com</td>
  </tr>
</table>
</center>
</body>
</html>
```

Listing 5.8 The Text of an HTML Document

Figure 5.1   The Display Created from the HTML

The `MyHtmlHandler` in Listing 5.7 is called by the SAX parser as it reads through the XML document in Listing 5.3. All of the information is stored in an array of `Person` objects. The `endDocument()` method is called at the end of the SAX parse operation, where the list is sorted and output as an HTML document. The names, telephone numbers, and email addresses are used as the text entries in an HTML table. The text of the HTML document is shown in Listing 5.8 and the resulting display is shown in Figure 5.1.

Summary

This chapter, and the one before it, explored the things that can be done with the SAX parser and the techniques for doing them. Although SAX is ideal for tasks that translate a document from XML into some other form, or for tasks that use a simple set of rules for extracting data from XML, the parser can also act as the front end to a much more complex operation. An application can use the SAX parser as a convenience to verify the syntactic correctness of a document as it breaks it down into small usable pieces. The application could then store all of the pieces from the input into a memory-resident form that provides access to the pieces, and the program could then use scan and lookup techniques to randomly access the data to move freely from one place to another in the document. That is the subject of the next chapter. The DOM parser uses SAX as a front end to translate the document into a memory resident tree with each node of the tree corresponding to a type of data found in the document.

CHAPTER

6

DOM Document Parse and Read

This chapter shows how to use a DOM parser to read an XML document. A DOM parser loads the entire document into a memory-resident tree structure so that the nodes of the tree can be randomly accessed by an application program. The entire content of the XML document is contained in the nodes of the tree, and the nodes are all linked together in parent/child relationships that are representative of the relationships in the original document. The examples presented in this chapter demonstrate how to set up a DOM parser to read a document, how to check for errors while a document is being read, and how an application can move from one tree node to another to retrieve the pieces of the parsed document. Finally, the last example in the chapter demonstrates the methods required to extract information from each of the tree nodes.

A DOM tree can also be used to create and modify documents, but this chapter only concerns itself with the Java methods for reading XML documents into a DOM tree. There are many methods in the JAXP that can be used to create nodes and make other modifications to an existing parse tree, and all of these are explored in the next chapter.

A DOM Error Checker

The program in Listing 6.1 is the simplest possible DOM application. All it does is create a DOM parse tree. Although it does actually parse the XML document input to it, it doesn't do anything other than report any errors found while parsing the input, and

```java
import javax.xml.parsers.DocumentBuilder;
import javax.xml.parsers.DocumentBuilderFactory;
import org.w3c.dom.Document;
import org.xml.sax.InputSource;
import org.xml.sax.SAXException;
import javax.xml.parsers.ParserConfigurationException;
import java.io.*;

public class DOMCheck {
    static public void main(String[] arg) {
        String filename = null;
        boolean validate = false;

        if(arg.length == 1) {
            filename = arg[0];
        } else if(arg.length == 2) {
            if(!arg[0].equals("-v"))
                usage();
            validate = true;
            filename = arg[1];
        } else {
            usage();
        }

        // Create a new factory to create parsers that will
        // be aware of namespaces and will validate or
        // not according to the flag setting.
        DocumentBuilderFactory dbf =
DocumentBuilderFactory.newInstance();
        dbf.setValidating(validate);
        dbf.setNamespaceAware(true);

        // Use the factory to create a parser (builder) and use
        // it to parse the document.
        try {
            DocumentBuilder builder = dbf.newDocumentBuilder();
            builder.setErrorHandler(new MyErrorHandler());
            InputSource is = new InputSource(filename);
            Document doc = builder.parse(is);
        } catch (SAXException e) {
            System.exit(1);
        } catch (ParserConfigurationException e) {
            System.err.println(e);
            System.exit(1);
        } catch (IOException e) {
            System.err.println(e);
            System.exit(1);
        }
    }
    private static void usage() {
        System.err.println("Usage: DOMCheck [-v] <filename>");
        System.exit(1);
    }
}
```

Listing 6.1   Using DOM for Syntax Checking

the only reason it does that much is because the error reporting is built into the DOM parser.

You may notice that the `DOMCheck` program in Listing 6.1 is very similar to the `SAXCheck` program shown in Listing 4.2. Both programs do the same thing—check for syntax errors—except the one in Chapter 4 uses the SAX API to interface with the application, and the one in this chapter uses DOM. In both examples there is a factory object retrieved by a call to a static method, and the factory is then used to create the actual parser.

There is a good reason for the similarity between the two programs: Internally, in the JAXP, the DOM parser uses a SAX parser to read the incoming XML document and break it down into its component parts. Then, the DOM parser analyses the relationships among the parts of the document and organizes the components into a tree. The resulting DOM tree is held in memory in a form that can be traversed in any order by your application.

DocumentBuilderFactory

In Listing 6.1, the `DocumentBuilderFactory` has two of its options specifically set before the factory itself is created. A call is made to the method `setValidating()` to set the validation flag according to the option specified on the command line. The `setNamespaceAware()` method is called with a `true` argument so that the DOM parser will properly process namespace names for both the DTD and the element tag names.

A call is made to the static method `newInstance()` to create a new `Document-BuilderFactory` object. To do this, the method takes the following steps until a `DocumentBuilderFactory` is found:

1. If the system property `javax.xml.parsers.DocumentBuilderfactory` is set, its value is used as the class name of the returned object. This property can be stored as a persistent system property. Also, this property can be set from inside your program before the call to `newInstance()`, so you could use this technique to select from among a group of available parser factories. For more on managing properties, see java.util.Properties in the Java API documentation included as part of the documentation with your Java installation.

2. If it exists, the file named `lib/jaxp.properties` is read for the name of the class. The text of this file is in the standard Java properties format (see java.util.Properties in the Java API documentation). If the file contains a definition for the property key `java.xml.parsers.DocumentBuilderFactory`, its value is used. This is another technique you could use to select from among a group of parser factories.

3. If the JAR Services API is available, the available jar files will be searched for the class `META-INF/services/javax.xml.parsers.DocumentBuilderFactory`.

4. The default `DocumentBuilderFactory` of the JAXP is used.

If an instantiation error is encountered at any one of these steps, or if the default factory cannot be used for some reason, a `FactoryConfigurationError` is thrown.

There are some methods in the factory that can be used to preset certain configurations of the `DocumentBuilder` objects it produces. Two of these are used in the example in Listing 6.1—the ones described earlier that specify that the parsers the factory produces should perform validation and be aware of namespaces. The following is a list of the available option methods, each of which take a true or false argument:

`setCoalescing()`	If `true`, any output `CDATA` nodes that are adjacent to a text node will be combined with the text node to produce a single text node. If `false`, which is the default, `CDATA` nodes will appear as separate nodes.
`setExpandEntity` `References()`	If `true`, the parser will expand entities, replacing them with the text that is defined for them. If `false`, the entities will be unchanged. The default is `true`.
`setIgnoringComments()`	If `true`, the parser will completely ignore comments. If comments are not ignored, the parser will include each one as a node in the resulting parse tree. The default is `false`.
`setIgnoringElement` `ContentWhitespace()`	If `true`, the parser will use the element definitions of the DTD to detect whitespace inside elements that is not an actual part of the textual content of the element and will simply discard such whitespace. Setting this option to `true` requires that `setValidating()` also be set to `true`, otherwise the DTD is simply ignored. The default is `false`.
`setNamespaceAware()`	If `true`, the parser will detect the colon character in names and use it as a separator between a namespace name and a tag name. If `false`, which is the default, a colon character is simply treated as a normal character in a tag name.
`setValidating()`	If `true`, the parser will validate the document. The default is `false`.

DocumentBuilder

A `DocumentBuilder` object is a DOM parser. This class can reasonably be named `DocumentBuilder` because the result of the parse is a `Document` object. The creation of an actual parser is the result of a call to the method `newDocumentBuilder()` of the factory.

Actually, a `DocumentBuilder` is more than a parser. It can construct a `Document` object by parsing an XML document, and it can also be used to create new (empty) `Document` objects that can then be used as a shell for the construction of XML documents.

In the example in Listing 6.1, the call to `setErrorHandler()` specifies which error handler is to be used to process the errors. Because these errors are issued from SAX, this program uses the same error handler that was developed and described in Chapter 4. The `try/catch` block fields respond to `SAXException` and `IOException`, the same as the SAX application. There is also `catch` block that is prepared to catch a `ParserConfigurationException`, which is thrown to indicate that there is something seriously wrong with the parser (not with the XML program it is parsing).

There are five `parse()` methods in the `DocumentBuilder` class. They all parse an XML document and return a `Document` object, but each one reads its input from a different source. The input can be from a local file, an `InputSource` (as in the example), a standard Java input stream, or a location on the Internet (specified by its URI).

Document

A `Document` object is the root of the tree that results from the parse. The `Document` interface, which defines methods that provide access to the data it contains, is an extension of the `Node` interface. The `Node` interface defines methods for identifying the type of node and for locating a child, sibling, or parent node. There are also methods that can be used to modify the parse tree by doing things such as inserting and deleting nodes.

In the program in Listing 6.1 the `Document` object is ignored because the entire program has been written to only check an XML document for errors, so once the parsing is complete, there is nothing else to do.

The Shape of the DOM Parse Tree

The result of the input of an XML document is a parse tree represented by a `Document` object. The `Document` object, along with all the other nodes of the tree, implements the `Node` interface. It is the `Node` interface that defines the methods used to navigate through the tree.

The nodes have family relationships, and the navigation methods move from one relation to the another according to each one's relationship with the *current* node. That is, whenever you call one of the navigation methods, the node (or nodes) returned is the one that relates to the current `Node` object.

The current node may have one or more *child* nodes. A child node is one level farther from the root of the tree and refers the current node as its *parent* node. A node may have any number of child nodes, but it can only have one parent.

Nodes that have the same parent are called *siblings*. The siblings have an order that is determined by the order in which they appeared in the original XML document. Because these node relationships represent the order of a document, this order is considered to be important and is carefully maintained in the parse tree.

Each member of the tree, including the `Document` object at the root, implements the `org.w3c.dom.Node` interface, and the methods of this interface are the ones you use to move from one tree node to another. The methods defined in the `Node` interface are

Table 6.1   Parse Tree Navigation Methods of `org.w3c.dom.Node`

METHOD	RETURN TYPE	DESCRIPTION
`getChildNodes()`	`NodeList`	The returned list contains all of the child nodes of the current node. If there are no child nodes, the returned `NodeList` is empty.
`getFirstChild()`	`Node`	The returned node is the first child node of the current node. If there are no children, the return is `null`.
`getLastChild()`	`Node`	The returned node is the last child node of the current node. If there are no children, the return is `null`.
`getNextSibling()`	`Node`	The returned node is the next child (after the current node) of the parent node. If there is no next child, the return is `null`.
`getParentNode()`	`Node`	The returned node is the parent of the current node.
`getPreviousSibling()`	`Node`	The returned node is the previous child (before the current node) of the parent node. If there is no previous child, the return is `null`.

summarized in Table 6.1. As explained later in this chapter under "Node Types," some of the specific node types have special navigation methods of their own, but all nodes have the methods listed in Table 6.1.

It's probably worthwhile to mention that there are some special cases. There are three Node types that do not use the navigation methods and relationships described here. The Attr, Entity, and Notation node types exist only in lists inside other nodes. They are defined as Node types only for convenience, but they don't work the same way. It could be argued that they should have been constructed differently, but it causes no problem other than some slight confusion at first. It is convenient to have them the same type, as you will see later in this chapter.

A DOM Parse Tree Lister

Listing 6.2 is a program that uses DOM to parse an XML document into a tree and then uses the navigation methods to walk through the tree to list the nodes it finds.

The DOMDump program of Listing 6.2 is almost identical to the previous DOMCheck example in Listing 6.1, except the Document object produced from the parser is passed

```
import javax.xml.parsers.DocumentBuilder;
import javax.xml.parsers.DocumentBuilderFactory;
import org.w3c.dom.Document;
import org.xml.sax.InputSource;
import org.xml.sax.SAXException;
import javax.xml.parsers.ParserConfigurationException;
import java.io.*;

public class DOMDump {
    static public void main(String[] arg) {
        String filename = null;
        boolean validate = false;

        if(arg.length == 1) {
            filename = arg[0];
        } else if(arg.length == 2) {
            if(!arg[0].equals("-v"))
                usage();
            validate = true;
            filename = arg[1];
        } else {
            usage();
        }

        DocumentBuilderFactory dbf =
DocumentBuilderFactory.newInstance();
        dbf.setValidating(validate);
        dbf.setNamespaceAware(true);
        dbf.setIgnoringElementContentWhitespace(true);

        // Parse the input to produce a parse tree with its root
        // in the form of a Document object
        Document doc = null;
        try {
            DocumentBuilder builder = dbf.newDocumentBuilder();
            builder.setErrorHandler(new MyErrorHandler());
            InputSource is = new InputSource(filename);
            doc = builder.parse(is);
        } catch (SAXException e) {
            System.exit(1);
        } catch (ParserConfigurationException e) {
            System.err.println(e);
            System.exit(1);
        } catch (IOException e) {
            System.err.println(e);
            System.exit(1);
        }

        // Use a TreeDumper to list the tree
        TreeDumper td = new TreeDumper();
        td.dump(doc);
```

Listing 6.2   Using the DOM Parser to Build a Document Tree   (*continues*)

```
    }
    private static void usage() {
        System.err.println("Usage: DOMCheck [-v] <filename>");
        System.exit(1);
    }
}
```

Listing 6.2   *(continued)*

to the dump() method of a TreeDumper object. The TreeDumper class is shown in Listing 6.3.

The TreeDumper class in Listing 6.3 just has one public method. That method accepts a Document object as its argument and calls an internal method named dumpLoop() that recursively descends the tree and prints the type of each node it finds.

The node returned from the parse() method in Listing 6.2 is the root of the entire parse tree. This tree root implements the Document interface, so it can be treated as a Document object. It can also be treated as a Node object because the Document interface extends the Node interface. Only the top-level node of the tree is also a Document object; each of the other nodes implements a different interface that represents its type. All of these different interfaces extend the Node interface, which simplifies the process of traversing the tree from inside an application.

Listing 6.3 lists nodes of the tree in a very simple way. It does nothing more than display the name of the type of each node. Following the switch/case statement, a call

```
import org.w3c.dom.Document;
import org.w3c.dom.Node;
import org.w3c.dom.NodeList;

public class TreeDumper {
    public void dump(Document doc) {
        dumpLoop((Node)doc,"");
    }
    private void dumpLoop(Node node,String indent) {
        switch(node.getNodeType()) {
        case Node.CDATA_SECTION_NODE:
            System.out.println(indent + "CDATA_SECTION_NODE");
            break;
        case Node.COMMENT_NODE:
            System.out.println(indent + "COMMENT_NODE");
            break;
        case Node.DOCUMENT_FRAGMENT_NODE:
            System.out.println(indent + "DOCUMENT_FRAGMENT_NODE");
            break;
        case Node.DOCUMENT_NODE:
```

Listing 6.3   A Class That Walks through a DOM Parse Tree   *(continues)*

```
                System.out.println(indent + "DOCUMENT_NODE");
                break;
        case Node.DOCUMENT_TYPE_NODE:
                System.out.println(indent + "DOCUMENT_TYPE_NODE");
                break;
        case Node.ELEMENT_NODE:
                System.out.println(indent + "ELEMENT_NODE");
                break;
        case Node.ENTITY_NODE:
                System.out.println(indent + "ENTITY_NODE");
                break;
        case Node.ENTITY_REFERENCE_NODE:
                System.out.println(indent + "ENTITY_REFERENCE_NODE");
                break;
        case Node.NOTATION_NODE:
                System.out.println(indent + "NOTATION_NODE");
                break;
        case Node.PROCESSING_INSTRUCTION_NODE:
                System.out.println(indent + "PROCESSING_INSTRUCTION_NODE");
                break;
        case Node.TEXT_NODE:
                System.out.println(indent + "TEXT_NODE");
                break;
        default:
                System.out.println(indent + "Unknown node");
                break;
        }

        NodeList list = node.getChildNodes();
        for(int i=0; i<list.getLength(); i++)
                dumpLoop(list.item(i),indent + "    ");


    }
}
```

Listing 6.3   *(continued)*

is made to getChildNode() to retrieve a complete list of the tree nodes that have the current node for a parent. The NodeList method getLength() returns a count, possibly zero, of the number of child nodes. The program then uses this count to loop once for each of the child nodes and makes a recursive call to dumpLoop() to descend the tree and display the name of the node and the name of all its children.

The XML document shown in Listing 6.4 is processed through DOMDump of Listing 6.2 to produce the output shown in Listing 6.5.

It is quite easy to see the relationship between Listings 6.4 and 6.5. The program indented the output in Listing 6.5 to indicate the parent and child relationship among the nodes. The root of the tree is the DOCUMENT_NODE, which contains all of the other nodes; it never has a sibling or a parent node. The next three nodes in the listing are the immediate Child nodes of the Document node. Each of the element nodes, defined in

```
<?xml version="1.0" standalone="yes"?>

<!-- This document is both well formed and valid -->

<!DOCTYPE folks [
<!ELEMENT folks (person)*>
<!ELEMENT person (name, phone, email)>
<!ELEMENT name (#PCDATA)>
<!ELEMENT phone (#PCDATA)>
<!ELEMENT email (#PCDATA)>
]>

<folks>
    <person>
        <name>Bertha D. Blues</name>
        <phone>907 555-8901</phone>
        <email>bertha@xyz.net</email>
    </person>
</folks>
```

Listing 6.4 A Well-Formed and Valid XML Document

XML as both an opening tag and a closing tag, is combined into a single ELEMENT_NODE in the parse tree. Also, the entire DTD is represented as a single node in the tree of the type DOCUMENT_TYPE_NODE.

Listing 6.6 is the result of dumping the same XML file as the one dumped in Listing 6.5, except whitespace is not being suppressed. Listing 6.6 shows the tree structure resulting from a parser gotten from a parser factory that did not have its whitespace suppression turned on by a call to setIgnoringElementContentWhitespace(). All of the extra TEXT_NODES in the listing are a result of the whitespace that was used to indent the code and to mark the ends of lines (the carriage return characters). As you can see, their inclusion adds a bit of confusion to the parse tree. The decorative whitespace is seldom useful, so the option to suppress it has been included as part of the parser.

```
DOCUMENT_NODE
    COMMENT_NODE
    DOCUMENT_TYPE_NODE
    ELEMENT_NODE
        ELEMENT_NODE
            ELEMENT_NODE
                TEXT_NODE
            ELEMENT_NODE
                TEXT_NODE
            ELEMENT_NODE
                TEXT_NODE
```

Listing 6.5 A Dump of the XML Document in Listing 6.4

```
DOCUMENT_NODE
    COMMENT_NODE
    DOCUMENT_TYPE_NODE
    ELEMENT_NODE
        TEXT_NODE
        ELEMENT_NODE
            TEXT_NODE
            ELEMENT_NODE
                TEXT_NODE
            TEXT_NODE
            ELEMENT_NODE
                TEXT_NODE
            TEXT_NODE
            ELEMENT_NODE
                TEXT_NODE
            TEXT_NODE
        TEXT_NODE
```

Listing 6.6   A Dump of the XML in Listing 6.4 without Whitespace Suppression

A Detailed Parse Tree Dumper

Each node in a DOM parse tree contains the information that is specific to that type of node. Not only are there tree nodes describing the XML document itself, but there are also nodes that contain much of the information from the DTD.

Listing the Contents of Parse Tree Nodes

The class shown in Listing 6.7 contains the method dumpLoop(), which traverses the parse tree and displays the information contained in each of the nodes it finds. This program is in the same basic form as the one in Listing 6.3, but in this version, instead of simply listing each node type, a method is called to display the contents of each specific node type.

To execute the class in Listing 6.7, the program shown in Listing 6.2 can be used by changing the last two lines of the main() method to the following:

```
TreeDumper2 td = new TreeDumper2();
td.dump(doc);
```

The method dumpLoop() accepts a Node object as its argument and uses a switch statement to call the correct method for the node type. Listing 6.8 is an XML document devised to demonstrate the form of the output from this program, which is shown as Listing 6.9.

```
import org.w3c.dom.Attr;
import org.w3c.dom.CDATASection;
import org.w3c.dom.Comment;
import org.w3c.dom.Document;
import org.w3c.dom.DocumentType;
import org.w3c.dom.DocumentFragment;
import org.w3c.dom.Element;
import org.w3c.dom.Entity;
import org.w3c.dom.EntityReference;
import org.w3c.dom.NamedNodeMap;
import org.w3c.dom.Node;
import org.w3c.dom.NodeList;
import org.w3c.dom.Notation;
import org.w3c.dom.ProcessingInstruction;
import org.w3c.dom.Text;

public class TreeDumper2 {
    public void dump(Document doc) {
        dumpLoop((Node)doc,"");
    }
    private void dumpLoop(Node node,String indent) {
        switch(node.getNodeType()) {
        case Node.ATTRIBUTE_NODE:
            dumpAttributeNode((Attr)node,indent);
            break;
        case Node.CDATA_SECTION_NODE:
            dumpCDATASectionNode((CDATASection)node,indent);
            break;
        case Node.COMMENT_NODE:
            dumpCommentNode((Comment)node,indent);
            break;
        case Node.DOCUMENT_NODE:
            dumpDocument((Document)node,indent);
            break;
        case Node.DOCUMENT_FRAGMENT_NODE:
            dumpDocumentFragment((DocumentFragment)node,indent);
            break;
        case Node.DOCUMENT_TYPE_NODE:
            dumpDocumentType((DocumentType)node,indent);
            break;
        case Node.ELEMENT_NODE:
            dumpElement((Element)node,indent);
            break;
        case Node.ENTITY_NODE:
            dumpEntityNode((Entity)node,indent);
            break;
        case Node.ENTITY_REFERENCE_NODE:
            dumpEntityReferenceNode((EntityReference)node,indent);
            break;
        case Node.NOTATION_NODE:
            dumpNotationNode((Notation)node,indent);
            break;
```

Listing 6.7   Using the DOM Parser to Extract XML Document Data   (*continues*)

```
        case Node.PROCESSING_INSTRUCTION_NODE:
            dumpProcessingInstructionNode(
                    (ProcessingInstruction)node,indent);
            break;
        case Node.TEXT_NODE:
            dumpTextNode((Text)node,indent);
            break;
        default:
            System.out.println(indent + "Unknown node");
            break;
        }

        NodeList list = node.getChildNodes();
        for(int i=0; i<list.getLength(); i++)
            dumpLoop(list.item(i),indent + "    ");
}

/* Display the contents of a ATTRIBUTE_NODE */
private void dumpAttributeNode(Attr node,String indent) {
    System.out.println(indent + "ATTRIBUTE " + node.getName() +
            "=\"" + node.getValue() + "\"");
}

/* Display the contents of a CDATA_SECTION_NODE */
private void dumpCDATASectionNode(CDATASection node,String indent) {
    System.out.println(indent + "CDATA SECTION length=" +
            node.getLength());
    System.out.println(indent + "\"" + node.getData() + "\"");
}

/* Display the contents of a COMMENT_NODE */
private void dumpCommentNode(Comment node,String indent) {
    System.out.println(indent + "COMMENT length=" + node.getLength());
    System.out.println(indent + "  " + node.getData());
}

/* Display the contents of a DOCUMENT_NODE */
private void dumpDocument(Document node,String indent) {
    System.out.println(indent + "DOCUMENT");
}

/* Display the contents of a DOCUMENT_FRAGMENT_NODE */
private void dumpDocumentFragment(DocumentFragment node,
            String indent) {
    System.out.println(indent + "DOCUMENT FRAGMENT");
}

/* Display the contents of a DOCUMENT_TYPE_NODE */
private void dumpDocumentType(DocumentType node,String indent) {
    System.out.println(indent + "DOCUMENT_TYPE: " + node.getName());
    if(node.getPublicId() != null)
```

Listing 6.7   (continues)

```
            System.out.println(indent +
                    " Public ID: " + node.getPublicId());
    if(node.getSystemId() != null)
        System.out.println(indent +
                " System ID: " + node.getSystemId());

    NamedNodeMap entities = node.getEntities();
    if(entities.getLength() > 0) {
        for(int i=0; i<entities.getLength(); i++) {
            dumpLoop(entities.item(i),indent + "  ");
        }
    }

    NamedNodeMap notations = node.getNotations();
    if(notations.getLength() > 0) {
        for(int i=0; i<notations.getLength(); i++)
            dumpLoop(notations.item(i),indent + "  ");
    }
}

/* Display the contents of a ELEMENT_NODE */
private void dumpElement(Element node,String indent) {
    System.out.println(indent + "ELEMENT: " + node.getTagName());
    NamedNodeMap nm = node.getAttributes();
    for(int i=0; i<nm.getLength(); i++)
        dumpLoop(nm.item(i),indent + "  ");
}

/* Display the contents of a ENTITY_NODE */
private void dumpEntityNode(Entity node,String indent) {
    System.out.println(indent + "ENTITY: " + node.getNodeName());
}

/* Display the contents of a ENTITY_REFERENCE_NODE */
private void dumpEntityReferenceNode(EntityReference node,
            String indent) {
    System.out.println(indent + "ENTITY REFERENCE: " +
            node.getNodeName());
}

/* Display the contents of a NOTATION_NODE */
private void dumpNotationNode(Notation node,String indent) {
    System.out.println(indent + "NOTATION");
    System.out.print(indent + "  " + node.getNodeName() + "=");
    if(node.getPublicId() != null)
        System.out.println(node.getPublicId());
    else
        System.out.println(node.getSystemId());
}

/* Display the contents of a PROCESSING_INSTRUCTION_NODE */
private void dumpProcessingInstructionNode(
            ProcessingInstruction node,String indent) {
```

Listing 6.7   *(continues)*

```
        System.out.println(indent + "PI: target=" + node.getTarget());
        System.out.println(indent + "   " + node.getData());
    }

    /* Display the contents of a TEXT_NODE */
    private void dumpTextNode(Text node, String indent) {
        System.out.println(indent + "TEXT length=" + node.getLength());
        System.out.println(indent + "   " + node.getData());
    }
}
```

Listing 6.7   (continued)

Each of the node types is defined in JAXP as an interface, and each of these interfaces extends the base interface org.w3c.dom.Node. This means that although each node of the tree can be of a different type, every one of them can also be treated as either a Node object or as an object of its specific type. Treating each one as a Node type allows for standard code to traverse the tree, and then each one is cast to its own type to provide access to all of its methods.

Whether child, parent, or sibling nodes exist depends on the type of the current node. For example, some of the node types exist only as children of other nodes and never have children or siblings of their own. In some circumstances nodes do not have parent nodes. (These nodes are generally stored in an array of nodes within another node.) In other words, even though the Node interface defines a standard set of methods for each of them, the actual traversal of the tree has to be done, to some extent, according to the node type.

DOM Parse Tree Node Types

Each of the following sections briefly describes a node type and the data that can be retrieved from each one when reading an XML document. There are also methods that can be used to store information in each node—to edit the information in the parse tree—but this chapter only concerns itself with parsing and reading an XML document.

The Attr Node

An Attr node contains a single attribute definition for an Element node. There are only two pieces of information required for an attribute: the attribute name and its value. In the method dumpAttributeNode() in Listing 6.7 the methods getName() and getValue() are called to return the two strings. If an attribute has been defined for an element but has not been assigned a value, and it does not have a default value in the DTD, it will not appear in the list; that is, every Attr node will return non-null values for both getName() and getValue().

Because an Attr node can only exist as the member of a list inside an Element node, an Attr node can never appear as a node in the parse tree. Therefore, the Attr nodes have no siblings and no parent.

```
<?xml version="1.0" standalone="yes"?>

<!-- Test XML for DOM node lister -->

<?scrollwin height="34" width="72"?>

<!DOCTYPE contact [
<!ELEMENT contact (phone | address)*>
<!ELEMENT address (#PCDATA)>
<!ELEMENT phone (#PCDATA)>
<!ATTLIST phone extension CDATA #IMPLIED>
<!ATTLIST phone location CDATA #IMPLIED>
<!ATTLIST phone id ID #IMPLIED>
<!NOTATION jpeg PUBLIC "JPEG">
<!NOTATION pin SYSTEM "http:/www.belugalake.com/xbox/pinlbl.txt">
<!ENTITY company "International Widget">
]>

<contact>
    <phone>907 555-8901</phone>
    <phone id="fred">907 555-0821</phone>
    <phone location="local">555-3401</phone>
    <phone location="work" extension="910">555-0332</phone>
    <address><![CDATA[
    1313 Blueview Terrace
    Sicard, Louisiana 77502]]></address>
    <address>Mail stop 34 at &company;</address>
</contact>
```

Listing 6.8   Example Document Containing a Variety of XML Types

The CDATASection Node

A CDATASection node contains the preformatted CDATA text that has been included as part (or all) of the text of an element. This node type is actually an extension of the Text node and adds no method definitions of its own. As a result, as far as reading an XML document is concerned, you can treat the contents of a CDATASection node the same as you would a Text node. The only real difference between the two of them occurs in the form in which the text is written in the source XML document. Although normal XML text is parsed and possibly modified by the XML parser, every character of the text inside a CDATA section is preserved exactly as written, including carriage returns and tabs.

The CDATASection interface extends Text, which in turn, extends the Character-Data interface. It is the CharacterData interface that defines the methods getLength() and getData() used in the dumpCDATASectionNode() of Listing 6.7.

If the setCoalescing() option has been set in the parser (as described earlier in this chapter, under "DocumentBuilderFactory"), each CDATASection node will have been merged with any adjacent Text nodes, resulting in a single Text node containing all the text.

```
DOCUMENT
   COMMENT length=30
      Test XML for DOM node lister
   PI: target=scrollwin
      height="34" width="72"
   DOCUMENT_TYPE: contact
      ENTITY: company
      NOTATION
         jpeg=JPEG
      NOTATION
         pin=http:/www.belugalake.com/xbox/pinlbl.txt
   ELEMENT: contact
      ELEMENT: phone
         TEXT length=12
            907 555-8901
      ELEMENT: phone
        ATTRIBUTE id="fred"
         TEXT length=12
            907 555-0821
      ELEMENT: phone
        ATTRIBUTE location="local"
         TEXT length=8
            555-3401
      ELEMENT: phone
        ATTRIBUTE location="work"
        ATTRIBUTE extension="910"
         TEXT length=8
            555-0332
      ELEMENT: address
         CDATA SECTION length=52
         "
1313 Blueview Terrace
Sicard, Louisiana 77502"
      ELEMENT: address
         TEXT length=36
            Mail stop 34 at International Widget
```

Listing 6.9 Output Resulting from Dumping Listing 6.8

The Comment *Node*

The Comment node contains the text of a comment found in the XML document. The text is included without the leading `<!--` and the trailing `-->`. This node adds no method definitions of its own beyond those it inherits from the CharacterData interface. It is the CharacterData interface that defines the methods getLength() and getData() used in the dumpCommentNode() of Listing 6.7.

You can use the setIgnoringComments() method, described earlier in this chapter (see "DocumentBuilderFactory"), to instruct the parser to discard the comments and cause none of these nodes to appear in the tree.

The Document *Node*

There is only one Document node, and it is the root of the tree. Starting with this node, it is possible to reach every node in the parse tree.

The Document node defines some convenience methods that can be used for direct access to other portions of the parse tree. None of these methods are used in the example in Listing 6.7 because the entire tree is traversed, which means it visits all the nodes. There is a method named getDocType() that you can use to directly retrieve the DocumentType node and another method named getDocumentElement() that will retrieve the root Element node. The method getElementsByTagName() can be used to retrieve a list of all the actual elements defined using the specified tag name. For example, the following line of code will retrieve an ordered list of all phone elements in the entire parse tree:

```
NodeList list = documentNode.getElementsByTagName("phone");
```

If your XML document is using namespaces, you can use the method get-ElementsByTagNameNS() to specify both the namespace and name of the tag, like this:

```
NodeList list = documentNod.getElementsByTagNameNS("namespace","tag");
```

The method named getElementById() can be used to retrieve an Element node by its ID. The following example shows how to directly retrieve the Element node that contains the ID string "fred" shown in Listing 6.8.

```
Element elem = documentNode.getElementById("fred");
```

If there is no element with an ID of "fred" in the parse tree, the return is null. If there is more than one element with the same ID string, the result is undetermined.

The DocumentFragment *Node*

A DocumentFragment node is almost the same as a Document node. However, it is stored internally in the parse tree, not at the root. Nodes of this type can be created and manipulated by programs that edit the parse tree. You will not encounter one of these nodes when you are reading a document.

The DocumentType *Node*

A DocumentType node contains the information from the DTD. Unlike most of the other nodes, this portion of the parse tree cannot be edited, so this node type contains only methods that can be used to read information.

Each document type is defined as being either SYSTEM or PUBLIC, so depending on which type it is, the defining string can be returned from either getSystemId() or getPublicId(). In every case, one will return a string and the other will return null.

Although this node is included as an integral part of the parse tree, it actually has no child nodes, which means the structure of the DTD is not available through the normal tree traversal methods. That is, at the bottom of the method dumpLoop() in Listing 6.7, the call to getChildNodes() will always return a zero-length list for the Document-Type node. The DocumentType node actually does have child nodes, but it keeps them private, and you can only locate them through the method calls getEntities()

and getNotations(). There is an example of each of these in the dumpDocument-
Type() method in Listing 6.7.

The Element *Node*

There is one Element node in the parse tree for each element found in the XML document. The content of the element (the data between the opening and closing tags) is
included as part of the parse tree as a child of its containing Element node. This
means that the only information included in an Element node object is the name of the
tag and any attributes that have been defined for it. As shown in the method
dumpElement() of Listing 6.7, the name of the element is returned from a call to
getTagName() and the attributes are returned from a call to getAttributes().

The getAttributes() method returns a NamedNodeMap object, which contains a
list of Attr objects. Each Attr object is a node containing one of the attributes associated with the element. The NamedNodeMap object contains a list of Node objects keyed
with names, which makes it easy for a program to retrieve the value of an attribute by
using the attribute name. In the dumpElement() method of Listing 6.7, a loop is used
to read sequentially through the list of Attr objects, and the dumpLoop() method is
called to display each one.

The Entity *Node*

An Entity node is a container for the name of an entity. This name can be retrieved by a
call to getNodeName(). It is also possible that the entity was declared as either PUBLIC
or SYSTEM, so there are the methods getPublicId() and getSystemId() that will return these strings. Both of these methods will return null if there was no such declaration.

This node type is not part of the general parse tree; it is stored as a member of a list
in the DocumentType node. This means that an Entity node has no siblings and no
parent.

The EntityReference *Node*

An EntityReference node may be used where, in the text, there is a reference to a previously defined entity. You may never actually encounter a node of this type. It is more
common for the textual substitution of the entity to be made and the result parsed as a line
of text. An example of this treatment is shown for the entity named company that is defined in the DTD of the XML document in Listing 6.8. At the bottom of the example document there is a reference to the company entity inside the text of an address element.
Then, as shown at the bottom of Listing 6.9, instead of an EntityReference node, there
is simply the text of the element with the expanded entity text inserted into the line.

You can control whether or not entities are expanded into text or appear as nodes by
using the setExpandEntityReferences() option setting method, as described in
the section "DocumentBuilderFactory," earlier in this chapter. If the purpose
of your application is to make simple modifications to an XML document, and it is
possible that the value of the entity value could be modified before the new document
is used, you would want to inhibit the expansion of entities so that you could restore
the document to its original state.

The `Notation` *Node*

A `Notation` node contains the declaration data of a DTD notation. As shown in the `dumpNotationNode()` method of Listing 6.8, the name of the notation can be retrieved by a call to `getNodeName()`, and the string it is associated with is returned from `getPublic-Id()` if the notation is `PUBLIC` or from `getSystemId()` if the declaration is `SYSTEM`.

This node type is not part of the general parse tree; it is a child of the `DocumentType` node. Because `Notation` nodes exist only inside `DocumentType` nodes, they never appear as a node in the parse tree. This means that the `Notation` nodes have no siblings and no parent.

The `ProcessingInstruction` *Node*

A `ProcessingInstruction` node contains the text of a processing instruction found in the XML document. It provides the methods `getTarget()`, which returns the name of the instruction, and `getData()`, which returns the actual text of the instruction.

The XML document in Listing 6.8 contains a processing instruction with the target name of `scrollwin`. The method named `dumpProcessingInstruction()` in Listing 6.7 prints the two strings, and as you can see in the output shown in Listing 6.9, all of the text following the target name is displayed without being modified. The format of the text is completely ignored by the DOM parser because it is assumed that the application will know what format to expect and know how to read it.

The `TextNode` *Node*

The `TextNode` interface is an extension of the `CharacterData` interface, so a `TextNode` object implements both the `getLength()` method, which returns a count of the number of characters in the text, and the `getData()` method, which returns the text itself.

Summary

This chapter is a demonstration of using a DOM parser to load an entire XML document into a memory-resident tree. During the parsing, any errors that are encountered are caught and displayed. The tree itself is composed of a collection of `Node` objects, each of which indicates its contents by the particular interface it implements. Once the parse tree is loaded, it can easily be traversed inside an application by using the methods that connect one node to another. There are some special nodes that are held in arrays inside other nodes, but most of them appear in parent, child, and sibling relationships in the parse tree. Each node type provides methods that can be used to extract its contained data. Most of these methods are described in this chapter, and there are examples showing how to traverse the tree and display the information found in each node.

Chapter 7 looks at the other side of DOM. Once a document has been loaded into a parse tree, that tree can be modified. New nodes can be inserted into the tree, old ones deleted, and the existing ones modified. After all this is done, the result can be output either as a modified XML document or in some entirely different form.

CHAPTER

7

Editing the DOM Parse Tree

This chapter is all about editing the RAM-resident form of the DOM parse tree of an XML document. DOM reads and loads an entire document, holding it in memory, so it can be dynamically edited and then written out in some other form (including XML). This chapter contains examples of how to use the DOM parse tree API to modify the internally held form of a document, and it then shows how to use the modified tree to produce a new XML document. This same procedure can also be used to create a brand new document either from scratch or from a template document.

The parse tree is only linked in one direction. That is, a parent node knows how to locate all of its children, but a child does not know how to locate its parent. This means that a process working with the DOM parse tree must keep track of its location if it wishes to retrace its steps. This is not a problem because an application can be designed to make a method call each time it descends the tree and only has to return from the method to return to its former location in the tree. Another consequence of this one-way relationship is that it's relatively easy to extract a portion of the tree and move it to another location, and it's also possible for a subtree to be placed simultaneously in more than one location in the tree. That is, a single node can have more than one parent.

Making a Copy of a Document

The program in Listing 7.1 is an example of the simplest form of document processing. It uses the DOM parser to read an XML document and then, from the information in

```
import javax.xml.parsers.DocumentBuilder;
import javax.xml.parsers.DocumentBuilderFactory;
import org.w3c.dom.Document;
import org.xml.sax.InputSource;
import org.xml.sax.SAXException;
import javax.xml.parsers.ParserConfigurationException;
import java.io.*;

public class DOMCopy {
    static public void main(String[] arg) {
        if(arg.length != 2) {
            System.err.println("Usage: DOMCopy <infile> <outfile>");
            System.exit(1);
        }
        DOMCopy dc = new DOMCopy();
        dc.inandout(arg[0],arg[1]);
    }
    public void inandout(String infile,String outfile) {
        DocumentBuilderFactory dbf =
DocumentBuilderFactory.newInstance();
        dbf.setValidating(true);
        dbf.setNamespaceAware(true);
        dbf.setIgnoringElementContentWhitespace(true);

        Document doc = null;
        try {
            DocumentBuilder builder = dbf.newDocumentBuilder();
            builder.setErrorHandler(new MyErrorHandler());
            InputSource is = new InputSource(infile);
            doc = builder.parse(is);
            // Code could be added here to modify the parse tree
            FileOutputStream fos = new FileOutputStream(outfile);
            TreeToXML ttxml = new TreeToXML();
            ttxml.write(fos,doc);
            fos.close();
        } catch (SAXException e) {
            System.exit(1);
        } catch (ParserConfigurationException e) {
            System.err.println(e);
            System.exit(1);
        } catch (IOException e) {
            System.err.println(e);
            System.exit(1);
        }

    }
}
```

Listing 7.1   Duplicate an XML Document without Change

the DOM parse tree, writes the element nodes of the parse tree into another XML document file. The class that writes the parse tree as an XML document is used as the basis for many of the examples in this chapter; it has the ability to parse an XML file into a tree and write from the tree to a file, so it can be used to demonstrate modifications made to the parse tree.

In Listing 7.1 there's a comment following the call to the parse() method. At the point where the comment appears, the entire XML document resides in memory and is available to your program. For most of the examples in this chapter, there are various method calls inserted at this point to demonstrate how changes can be made to the tree. There are two steps to each modification: First, find the location to be changed, and second, call the appropriate methods for making the change.

As for DOM parsing, nothing new has been added to the example programs developed in Chapter 6. The program uses the DocumentBuilderFactory to construct an instance of a DocumentBuilder and then uses the DocumentBuilder to create the parser used to load the XML file into a memory-resident parse tree. After the parse tree has been completed and returned from the parse() method in the form of a Document object, a TreeToXML object is created that writes the information from the parse tree into another file. Listing 7.2 is the TreeToXML class. Once a TreeToXML object has been constructed, it's capable of writing any number of parse trees by making repeated calls to the write() method with the output stream and a Document object, which is the root node of the parse tree.

```
import org.w3c.dom.Document;
import org.w3c.dom.DocumentType;
import org.w3c.dom.NodeList;
import org.w3c.dom.NamedNodeMap;
import org.w3c.dom.Node;
import org.w3c.dom.Element;
import org.w3c.dom.Attr;
import org.w3c.dom.Text;
import org.w3c.dom.CDATASection;
import org.w3c.dom.Comment;
import org.w3c.dom.ProcessingInstruction;
import java.io.*;

public class TreeToXML {
    private static final String TAB = "    ";
    private PrintWriter out;

    public void write(OutputStream stream,Document doc)
                throws IOException {
        out = new PrintWriter(stream);
        outputHeading(doc);
        outputElement(doc.getDocumentElement(),"");
        out.flush();
```

Listing 7.2   Creating an XML Document from a DOM Tree   (continues)

```
        }
    private void outputHeading(Document doc) {
        out.print("<?xml version=\"1.0\"");
        DocumentType doctype = doc.getDoctype();
        if(doctype != null) {
            if((doctype.getPublicId() == null) &&
                    (doctype.getSystemId() == null)) {
                out.println(" standalone=\"yes\"?>");
            } else {
                out.println(" standalone=\"no\"?>");
            }
        } else {
            out.println("?>");
        }
    }
    private void outputElement(Element node,String indent) {
        out.print(indent + "<" + node.getTagName());
        NamedNodeMap nm = node.getAttributes();
        for(int i=0; i<nm.getLength(); i++) {
            Attr attr = (Attr)nm.item(i);
            out.print(" " + attr.getName() + "=\"" +
                    attr.getValue() + "\"");
        }
        out.println(">");
        NodeList list = node.getChildNodes();
        for(int i=0; i<list.getLength(); i++)
            outputloop(list.item(i),indent + TAB);
        out.println(indent + "</" + node.getTagName() + ">");
    }
    private void outputText(Text node,String indent) {
        out.println(indent + node.getData());
    }
    private void outputCDATASection(CDATASection node,String indent) {
        out.println(indent + "<![CDATA[" + node.getData() + "]]>");
    }
    private void outputComment(Comment node,String indent) {
        out.println(indent + "<!-- " + node.getData() + " -->");
    }
    private void outputProcessingInstructionNode(
            ProcessingInstruction node,String indent) {
        out.println(indent + "<?" + node.getTarget() + " " +
                node.getData() + "?>");
    }

    private void outputloop(Node node,String indent) {
        switch(node.getNodeType()) {
        case Node.ELEMENT_NODE:
            outputElement((Element)node,indent);
            break;
        case Node.TEXT_NODE:
            outputText((Text)node,indent);
            break;
```

Listing 7.2   (continues)

```
            case Node.CDATA_SECTION_NODE:
                outputCDATASection((CDATASection)node,indent);
                break;
            case Node.COMMENT_NODE:
                outputComment((Comment)node,indent);
                break;
            case Node.PROCESSING_INSTRUCTION_NODE:
                outputProcessingInstructionNode(
                        (ProcessingInstruction)node,indent);
                break;
            default:
                out.println("Unknown node type: " + node.getNodeType());
                break;
            }
        }
    }
```

Listing 7.2   (*continued*)

Listing 7.3 is a source document that's processed through DOMCopy to produce the output listing shown in Listing 7.4. Although the xml processing instruction line is retained in the output, none of the DTD information is written to the output. The DTD is in the parse tree and could have been written, but there is seldom a need to do so


```
<?xml version="1.0" standalone="yes"?>

<!-- This document is both well formed and valid -->

<!DOCTYPE folks [
<!ELEMENT folks (person)*>
<!ELEMENT person (name, phone, email)>
<!ELEMENT name (#PCDATA | bold)*>
<!ELEMENT phone (#PCDATA)>
<!ELEMENT email (#PCDATA)>
<!ELEMENT bold (#PCDATA)>
]>

<folks>
    <person>
        <name>Victor Von <bold>Creator</bold> Frankenstein</name>
        <phone>907 555-8901</phone>
        <email>monster@igor.net</email>
    </person>
</folks>
```

Listing 7.3   The Source XML Document

```
<?xml version="1.0" standalone="yes"?>
<folks>
    <person>
        <name>
            Victor Von
            <bold>
                Creator
            </bold>
            Frankenstein
        </name>
        <phone>
            907 555-8901
        </phone>
        <email>
            monster@igor.net
        </email>
    </person>
</folks>
```

Listing 7.4   The Output from DOMCopy

```
public void appendPerson(Document doc,
            String name,String phone,String email) {
    Element personNode = doc.createElement("person");

    Element nameNode = doc.createElement("name");
    personNode.appendChild(nameNode);
    Text nametextNode = doc.createTextNode(name);
    nameNode.appendChild(nametextNode);

    Element phoneNode = doc.createElement("phone");
    personNode.appendChild(phoneNode);
    Text phonetextNode = doc.createTextNode(phone);
    phoneNode.appendChild(phonetextNode);

    Element emailNode = doc.createElement("email");
    personNode.appendChild(emailNode);
    Text emailtextNode = doc.createTextNode(email);
    emailNode.appendChild(emailtextNode);

    Element root = doc.getDocumentElement();
    root.appendChild(personNode);
}
```

Listing 7.5   A Method for Adding a New Entry to the End of a List

because the DTD information is read-only in a parse tree. It cannot be modified in any way, so there's seldom a need to reproduce it.

Inserting a New Element Node

The method named `appendPerson()` shown in Listing 7.5 will add a new node to the parse tree of the document shown in Listing 7.3. Actually, it adds several nodes to the tree and, when output again, results in the output shown in Listing 7.6. The purpose of the method is to add a new person to the contact list, so it's necessary to add a `person` node that contains `name`, `phone`, and `email` nodes. Notice that the code in this example (as with most of the examples in this chapter) is very specific to the format of the document; that is, it knows the exact layout of the `person` node and it also knows that it's located immediately beneath the root node.

```
<?xml version="1.0" standalone="yes"?>
<folks>
    <person>
        <name>
            Victor Von
            <bold>
                Creator
            </bold>
            Frankenstein
        </name>
        <phone>
            907 555-8901
        </phone>
        <email>
            monster@igor.net
        </email>
    </person>
    <person>
        <name>
            Lanny Simpson
        </name>
        <phone>
            907 555-1189
        </phone>
        <email>
            lanny@belugalake.com
        </email>
    </person>
</folks>
```

Listing 7.6   The Result of Appending an Element

The method createElement() in the Document class is used to create a new element with the tag name "person". It is then a matter of creating three more Element nodes and appending them as children to the "person" node. Each node is created by a call to createElement(). A call is made to appendChild() for each of them to be added as children to the new "person" node. Also, the method createTextNode() is called to create a Text node to be a child of each of the three new nodes. Finally, a call is made to getDocumentElement() to retrieve the root node (which, in this case, is a "folks" element), and a call to appendChild() is made to add the new "person" node to the retrieved node. As shown in Listing 7.6, the output of the tree after the edits, the newly added nodes have been inserted following any sibling nodes that were already attached to the parent node.

There is another method that can be used to add a child to a node. In the appendPerson() method of Listing 7.5, the method appendChild() is used to add the new node as the last child in the list. Modifying the method to look like the one in Listing 7.7 does the same thing, but it inserts the new node in front of the child node instead of behind it. This is done by calling the insertBefore() method and passing it both the new node to be added and the child node that is to be preceded by the new node. The result is shown in Listing 7.8.

```
public void insertPerson(Document doc,
            String name,String phone,String email) {
    Element personNode = doc.createElement("person");

    Element nameNode = doc.createElement("name");
    personNode.appendChild(nameNode);
    Text nametextNode = doc.createTextNode(name);
    nameNode.appendChild(nametextNode);

    Element phoneNode = doc.createElement("phone");
    personNode.appendChild(phoneNode);
    Text phonetextNode = doc.createTextNode(phone);
    phoneNode.appendChild(phonetextNode);

    Element emailNode = doc.createElement("email");
    personNode.appendChild(emailNode);
    Text emailtextNode = doc.createTextNode(email);
    emailNode.appendChild(emailtextNode);

    Element root = doc.getDocumentElement();
    Node firstChildNode = root.getFirstChild();
    root.insertBefore(personNode,firstChildNode);
}
```

Listing 7.7 A Method for Inserting a New Entry in a List

```
<?xml version="1.0" standalone="yes"?>
<folks>
    <person>
        <name>
            Lanny Simpson
        </name>
        <phone>
            907 555-1189
        </phone>
        <email>
            lanny@belugalake.com
        </email>
    </person>
    <person>
        <name>
            Victor Von
            <bold>
                Creator
            </bold>
             Frankenstein
        </name>
        <phone>
            907 555-8901
        </phone>
        <email>
            monster@igor.net
        </email>
    </person>
</folks>
```

Listing 7.8   The Result of Inserting an Element

Locating a Node and Modifying Text

The XML document in Listing 7.9 contains is a list of three names, each of which has an email address associated with it. The method in Listing 7.11 looks through the tree until it finds a match for the name and then updates the entry with a new email address. The result is shown in Listing 7.10.

Changing one particular email address means that it is necessary to use some criterion to locate the one to be changed. In the method of Listing 7.11 the name of the person is used to find the entry, and then the associated email address element is located and modified.

The newEmail() method in Listing 7.11 starts at the root of the tree with the call to getDocumentElement(). A call is made to getChildNodes(), which returns a NodeList object containing an array of all the nodes that are children of the root node.

```
<?xml version="1.0" standalone="yes"?>
<!DOCTYPE folks [
<!ELEMENT folks (person)*>
<!ELEMENT person (name | phone | email)*>
<!ELEMENT name (#PCDATA | bold)*>
<!ELEMENT phone (#PCDATA)>
<!ELEMENT email (#PCDATA)>
<!ELEMENT bold (#PCDATA)>
]>

<folks>
    <person>
        <name>Sam Spade</name>
        <email>samspade@beluglalake.com</email>
    </person>
    <person>
        <name>Sam Diamond</name>
        <email>samdiamond@beluglalake.com</email>
    </person>
    <person>
        <name>Sam Sonite</name>
        <email>samsonite@beluglalake.com</email>
    </person>
</folks>
```

Listing 7.9   Three Names with Email Addresses

The NodeList method getLength() is used to specify the count of an iteration over each child node, and the NodeList method item() is used to retrieve each node in the array. The first node is number 0, the second is 1, and so on, just as in a Java array. Every node that has children has a getChildNodes() method that will return a NodeList object that contains the children; the return will be null if there are no children.

Each "person" element node has its own list of children. In the example in Listing 7.11 it is assumed there are always two—the first child is a "name" element and the second is an "email" element. Inside the loop, a person node is extracted from the list, and then a list of its child nodes is extracted. The first child node is the name, so a Text node is extracted from it and the ASCII is tested for a match. If a match is made, the second node (the "email" node) for this person is extracted. It also contains a list with a single Text node, and a call is made to setData() to insert the new text into the node. It simply replaces whatever text was already there.

There is another approach to doing exactly the same thing. Instead of using arrays of child names, it is often easier to use the sibling relationships among the nodes. The alternate approach to the same problem is shown in Listing 7.12. Probably the first thing you notice about the alternate approach is the fact that it takes fewer statements. It's shorter because there's no need to extract all of the child elements in a NodeList. Instead, it's possible to directly retrieve the node you want. The approach you use depends on the shape of your parse tree, how much its shape can vary, and just what it is you are trying to do.

```
<?xml version="1.0" standalone="yes"?>
<folks>
    <person>
        <name>
            Sam Spade
        </name>
        <email>
            samspade@beluglalake.com
        </email>
    </person>
    <person>
        <name>
            Sam Diamond
        </name>
        <email>
            sammy@belugalake.com
        </email>
    </person>
    <person>
        <name>
            Sam Sonite
        </name>
        <email>
            samsonite@beluglalake.com
        </email>
    </person>
</folks>
```

Listing 7.10   Three Names with an Email Address Updated

```
public void newEmail(Document doc,String newname,String newemail) {
    Element root = doc.getDocumentElement();
    NodeList rootlist = root.getChildNodes();
    for(int i=0; i<rootlist.getLength(); i++) {
        Element person = (Element)rootlist.item(i);
        NodeList personlist = person.getChildNodes();
        Element name = (Element)personlist.item(0);
        NodeList namelist = name.getChildNodes();
        Text nametext = (Text)namelist.item(0);
        String oldname = nametext.getData();
        if(oldname.equals(newname)) {
            Element email = (Element)personlist.item(1);
            NodeList emaillist = email.getChildNodes();
            Text emailtext = (Text)emaillist.item(0);
            emailtext.setData(newemail);
        }
    }
}
```

Listing 7.11   Locate a Name and Change Its Email Address

```
public void newEmail(Document doc,String newname,String newemail) {
    Element root = doc.getDocumentElement();
    Element person = (Element)root.getFirstChild();
    while(person != null) {
        Element name = (Element)person.getFirstChild();
        Text nametext = (Text)name.getFirstChild();
        String oldname = nametext.getData();
        if(oldname.equals(newname)) {
            Element email = (Element)name.getNextSibling();
            Text emailtext = (Text)email.getFirstChild();
            emailtext.setData(newemail);
        }
        person = (Element)person.getNextSibling();
    }
}
```

Listing 7.12   Locating a Node by Using Siblings

The call to the method getFirstChild() in Listing 7.12 returns the same node you would get if you first acquired a NodeList object and then retrieved a node by calling item(0). The loop now, instead of using a counter, continues to loop until person is null. At the bottom of the loop the person reference is assigned the address of the sibling following the current one and, if there are no more, it results in person being null. If a match is found on the name, a call is made to getNextSibling() of the "name" node to retrieve the node following it, which is the email node. A call to the email node's getFirstChild() method returns the Text node, and setData() is called to insert the new address.

If you want, you can use the sibling relationships to go in the opposite direction. A call to the method getLastNode() returns the last node in the list of child nodes, and a call to getPreviousSibling() returns the node that comes before the current one. By using all four methods, it's possible to start at either end and then move back and forth through list of child nodes.

There's no significant advantage in using the set of methods or using the array in the NodeList object. The only advantage that a NodeList object has over these methods is that it makes it possible to jump directly to any sibling node by simply using an index number. As you can see, however, using the sibling relationships makes the code shorter and a bit easier to read.

There are some shortcomings in the example in Listing 7.12. Some things were left out on purpose to keep the example simple. The calls to person.getFirstChild() and item() assume that the child of the "person" node is a Text node, and that the Text node contains the entire name. It could be that there is something besides a simple Text node that needs to be dealt with. It could be some other type of character data or even another Element node tagging part or all of the text as "bold" or something. To allow for all of the possibilities, there must be code present that detects several different types of nodes. It just depends on what is allowed by the DTD.

```
public void deleteFirstElement(Document doc) {
    Element root = doc.getDocumentElement();
    Element child = (Element)root.getFirstChild();
    root.removeChild(child);
}
```

Listing 7.13   Delete the First Child of the Root Node

Deleting a Tree Node

To remove a node from the tree, you must have a reference to both the node you wish to remove and to the parent node to which it is attached. The method in Listing 7.13 locates the root node of the parse tree and removes the first child node from it. Using the XML document shown in Listing 7.9 as input, the result is shown in Listing 7.14.

The method in Listing 7.13 first locates the root node by calling getDocument-Element() and then locates the first child of the root by calling getFirstChild(). Knowing the parent and child, all that is necessary to remove the child is to call the removeChild() method of the parent node.

This is one of the really nice thing about Java. You can use the removeChild() method to remove an entire subtree that contains a number of child and grandchild nodes, and because you no longer reference them, they will eventually be gathered up by the garbage collector and recycled for you. There is no need to bother with deleting each node in the subtree you wish to prune.

```
<?xml version="1.0" standalone="yes"?>
<folks>
    <person>
        <name>
            Sam Diamond
        </name>
        <email>
            samdiamond@beluglalake.com
        </email>
    </person>
    <person>
        <name>
            Sam Sonite
        </name>
        <email>
            samsonite@beluglalake.com
        </email>
    </person>
</folks>
```

Listing 7.14   After Removing the First Child Node

If your purpose for removing the node is to insert it into another location, the re-moved child is the value returned from the `removeChild()` method, which means you can use it as an argument in a method that inserts it into another location. This has the effect of moving a node, which can be an entire subtree, from one location to another in a single statement. An example is:

```
newparent.appendChild(oldparent.removeChild(child));
```

Replacing a Tree Node

It's possible to use the `replaceChild()` method to remove a node and replace it with another one. To do this, you need to have a reference to the node you're replacing as well as a reference to its parent node. The new node can be one that you've created or one that you've pruned from another location in the tree by using `removeChild()`.

Applying the method in Listing 7.15 to the document shown in Listing 7.9 replaces the first "person" element with a new one. The result is shown in Listing 7.16.

```
public void replacePerson(Document doc,
           String name,String phone,String email) {
    Element newPersonNode = doc.createElement("person");

    Element nameNode = doc.createElement("name");
    newPersonNode.appendChild(nameNode);
    Text nametextNode = doc.createTextNode(name);
    nameNode.appendChild(nametextNode);

    Element phoneNode = doc.createElement("phone");
    newPersonNode.appendChild(phoneNode);
    Text phonetextNode = doc.createTextNode(phone);
    phoneNode.appendChild(phonetextNode);

    Element emailNode = doc.createElement("email");
    newPersonNode.appendChild(emailNode);
    Text emailtextNode = doc.createTextNode(email);
    emailNode.appendChild(emailtextNode);

    Element root = doc.getDocumentElement();
    Element oldPersonNode = (Element)root.getFirstChild();
    root.replaceChild(newPersonNode,oldPersonNode);
}
```

Listing 7.15 Replacing an Existing Node with a New One

```
<?xml version="1.0" standalone="yes"?>
<folks>
    <person>
        <name>
            Lanny Simpson
        </name>
        <phone>
            907 555-1189
        </phone>
        <email>
            lanny@belugalake.com
        </email>
    </person>
    <person>
        <name>
            Sam Diamond
        </name>
        <email>
            samdiamond@beluglalake.com
        </email>
    </person>
    <person>
        <name>
            Sam Sonite
        </name>
        <email>
            samsonite@beluglalake.com
        </email>
    </person>
</folks>
```

Listing 7.16   Output Resulting from Replacing a Subtree

The value returned from the call to replaceChild() is a reference to the node that was removed. This makes it possible, in a single statement, to move a subtree from one location to another while inserting a new node in the newly vacated location. An example is:

```
newParent.insertChild(origParent.replaceChild(newNode,origNode));
```

Locating Elements by Tag Name

It's possible to initiate a search through the parse tree, or a subtree, for elements with a specific tag name. All elements that match the name you specify are returned to you in the array inside a NodeList object. The method in Listing 7.17 searches for all elements

```
    private void makeNamelist(Document doc) {
        String names = null;
        Element root = doc.getDocumentElement();
        NodeList nameElements = root.getElementsByTagName("name");
        for(int i=0; i<nameElements.getLength(); i++) {
            Element name = (Element)nameElements.item(i);
            Text nametext = (Text)name.getFirstChild();
            if(names == null)
                names = nametext.getData();
            else
                names += ", " + nametext.getData();
        }
        Element namelist = doc.createElement("namelist");
        Text namelisttext = doc.createTextNode(names);
        namelist.appendChild(namelisttext);
        root.insertBefore(namelist,root.getFirstChild());
    }
}
```

Listing 7.17   Add an Element Containing All Names

with the tag "name" and uses them to create a single string containing all the names. From this string a new element node with the tag name "namelist" is constructed and inserted as a new element immediately following the root node. When the XML file in Listing 7.9 is processed through this method, the result is the output shown in Listing 7.18.

The method makeNamelist() calls the method getElementsByTagName() with the tag name of the Element nodes sought. The method getElementsByTagName() is included in every member of the tree, so it can be used to locate nodes by name in any portion of the tree; it searches the entire subtree beginning with the specified node. The method makeNamelist() then loops once for each Element in the list and uses the text it finds to construct a string named names that contains a comma-separated list of all the names it finds. After the name list has been constructed, an Element named "namelist" is created—with its single child being a Text node containing the string of names—and the new Element is inserted as the first child of the root node with a call to appendChild(). The result is shown in Listing 7.18

Duplicating a Portion of the Tree

There is a convenient method that can be used to duplicate a single node or an entire subtree. The newly created node has no parent, so it can simply be added to the tree wherever you would like.

When copying a node, you must specify whether you want a shallow copy or a deep copy. If you request a shallow copy, only a single node will be actually duplicated, but the copy will have exactly the same set of child nodes as the original. Because the same node can be in more than one location in the parse tree, there is no need to duplicate

```
<?xml version="1.0" standalone="yes"?>
<folks>
    <namelist>
        Sam Spade, Sam Diamond, Sam Sonite
    </namelist>
    <person>
        <name>
            Sam Spade
        </name>
        <email>
            samspade@beluglalake.com
        </email>
    </person>
    <person>
        <name>
            Sam Diamond
        </name>
        <email>
            samdiamond@beluglalake.com
        </email>
    </person>
    <person>
        <name>
            Sam Sonite
        </name>
        <email>
            samsonite@beluglalake.com
        </email>
    </person>
</folks>
```

Listing 7.18   A New Element Is Constructed from All the Names

things you are not going to modify. After a shallow copy, any modification made to the duplicated node's subtree will also take effect in the subtree of the original. On the other hand, if you execute a deep copy, every node (including all of the text) is copied, making the two subtrees completely independent of one another.

The method `duplicatePerson()` shown in Listing 7.19 copies a node by calling the `cloneNode()` method of the `Element` node to be duplicated. The call to `appendChild()`

```
public void duplicatePerson(Document doc) {
    Element root = doc.getDocumentElement();
    Element origPerson = (Element)root.getFirstChild();
    Element newPerson = (Element)origPerson.cloneNode(true);
    root.appendChild(newPerson);
}
```

Listing 7.19   Duplicate a Subtree

inserts the new node into the tree as a sibling of the node that was copied. The depth argument passed to appendChild() is true, which causes a deep copy to be made; had an argument of false been used, the copy would have been shallow. Using the XML document from Listing 7.3, the output is shown in Listing 7.20.

For the most part, cloning subtrees will result in a faithful reproduction. If, for example, you clone an Element that has attributes, all of the attributes will also be cloned. If you request a shallow copy, only the node being cloned is actually copied, with the exception that the attributes of the duplicated node are also duplicated. The DTD information is read-only anyway, so there is no real purpose in cloning any of it, but if you decide to clone it anyway, the result you get is implementation dependent.

```
<?xml version="1.0" standalone="yes"?>
<folks>
    <person>
        <name>
            Victor Von
            <bold>
                Creator
            </bold>
            Frankenstein
        </name>
        <phone>
            907 555-8901
        </phone>
        <email>
            monster@igor.net
        </email>
    </person>
    <person>
        <name>
            Victor Von
            <bold>
                Creator
            </bold>
            Frankenstein
        </name>
        <phone>
            907 555-8901
        </phone>
        <email>
            monster@igor.net
        </email>
    </person>
</folks>
```

Listing 7.20   The Result of Cloning a Section of the Parse Tree

Setting an Attribute

Adding an attribute to an `Element` node is simply a matter of calling the node's `setAttribute()` method with the name of the attribute and the text of its value. The method in Listing 7.21 adds an attribute to the `"person"` node of the parse tree of the document shown in Listing 7.3. The result is shown in Listing 7.22.

The `setAttribute()` method can be used to add a new attribute to an `Element` node or to change the value of a previously defined attribute. That is, if the specified attribute already exists, it will simply have its value changed.

```
public void addAttribute(Document doc) {
    Element root = doc.getDocumentElement();
    Element person = (Element)root.getFirstChild();
    person.setAttribute("company","CastleWorks");
}
```

Listing 7.21   Adding an Attribute to an Element

```
<?xml version="1.0" standalone="yes"?>
<folks>
    <person company="CastleWorks">
        <name>
            Victor Von
            <bold>
                Creator
            </bold>
            Frankenstein
        </name>
        <phone>
            907 555-8901
        </phone>
        <email>
            monster@igor.net
        </email>
    </person>
</folks>
```

Listing 7.22   An Element with a New Attribute

Deleting an Attribute

Attributes can be deleted from an Element. The XML document in Listing 7.23 includes an element with a pair of attributes defined for it; one is named "extension" and the other is named "dept". The method named delAtribute() shown in Listing 7.24 locates the Element in the parse tree with the attributes set and then calls the method removeAttribute() to delete them both. However, because of the definitions in the DTD, only one is actually deleted. As shown in Listing 7.25, the optional attribute "extension" is completely removed, but removing the "dept" attribute simply converts it to its default value.

```
<?xml version="1.0" standalone="yes"?>
<!DOCTYPE folks [
<!ELEMENT folks (person)*>
<!ELEMENT person (name | email)*>
<!ELEMENT name (#PCDATA)>
<!ELEMENT email (#PCDATA)>
<!ATTLIST person extension CDATA #IMPLIED
                 dept CDATA "staff">
]>

<folks>
    <person extension="3412" dept="medical">
        <name>Doctor Polidori</name>
        <email>deft@jerk.net</email>
    </person>
</folks>
```

Listing 7.23   An XML Document Containing Two Attributes

```
public void delAttribute(Document doc) {
    Element root = doc.getDocumentElement();
    Element person = (Element)root.getFirstChild();
    person.removeAttribute("extension");
    person.removeAttribute("dept");
}
```

Listing 7.24   Deleting Two Attributes

```
<?xml version="1.0" standalone="yes"?>
<folks>
    <person dept="staff">
        <name>
            Doctor Polidori
        </name>
        <email>
            deft@jerk.net
        </email>
    </person>
</folks>
```

Listing 7.25 Attribute Removal Returns the Default

Moving and Copying Attributes

Attribute nodes are similar to other nodes in the tree, but there's one important difference. They aren't linked into the parse tree the same way as other nodes; instead they are stored in a special array inside an Element node. It needs to be done this way because of the special treatment they receive for things like default values. As for editing the parse tree, it means that you cannot use the normal child and sibling tree relationships to move attributes from one place to another, but the process is still quite straightforward. The previous sections demonstrated how an attribute can be added or deleted, and this section will demonstrate how to use the information from the attribute of one Element to produce an attribute for another Element. With the information from the previous sections and this one, you should be able to do anything you'd like with an Attr node.

The method shown in Listing 7.26 demonstrates approaches you can take to copy an attribute from one element to another. An attribute is made up of two parts—the name of the attribute and its value—and you can get a copy of an attribute by retrieving an Attr object or by simply retrieving its value string. In either case you need to know the name of an attribute to be able to retrieve its value. If you need to retrieve attributes without knowing their names, the technique for doing so is shown in the program in Listing 6.7.

In Listing 7.26 the Attr node for the "dept" attribute is retrieved from personOne by a call to getAttributeNode() and stored in the local reference named deptAttr. The attribute is deleted from personOne with a call to removeAttributeNode(). Then, to retrieve the value assigned to the attribute, a call is made to the getValue() method of the Attr node. Using the attribute name string and its value string, the attribute and its value are set in the personOne and personTwo elements.

If all you want to do is get the value of an attribute, a call can be made to getAttribute(), as shown where both the "mail" and "title" attribute values are copied from personOne. Each of these two extracted attribute strings are then

```
public void dupAttributes(Document doc) {
    Element root = doc.getDocumentElement();
    Element personOne = (Element)root.getFirstChild();
    Element personTwo = (Element)personOne.getNextSibling();
    Element personThree = (Element)personTwo.getNextSibling();

    Attr deptAttr = personOne.getAttributeNode("dept");
    personOne.removeAttributeNode(deptAttr);
    String deptString = deptAttr.getValue();
    personTwo.setAttribute("dept",deptString);
    personThree.setAttribute("dept",deptString);

    String mailString = personOne.getAttribute("mail");
    personTwo.setAttribute("mail",mailString);

    String titleString = personOne.getAttribute("title");
    personOne.removeAttribute("title");
    personThree.setAttribute("title",titleString);
}
```

Listing 7.26 Copying Attributes

inserted into other `element` nodes in calls to `setAttribute()`. Also, the `"title"` attribute is removed from `personOne` with a call to `removeAttribute()`.

Applying this method to the XML document shown in Listing 7.27 will result in the document with the set of attributes shown in Listing 7.28.

You should be aware that removing an attribute will not succeed if the attribute is defined in the DTD as having a default value. In that case, instead of being deleted, the attribute will simply revert to the default value.

```
<?xml version="1.0" standalone="yes"?>
<!DOCTYPE folks [
<!ELEMENT folks (person)*>
<!ELEMENT person (name | email)*>
<!ELEMENT name (#PCDATA)>
<!ELEMENT email (#PCDATA)>
<!ELEMENT bold (#PCDATA)>
<!ATTLIST person floor CDATA #IMPLIED
                 dept CDATA #IMPLIED
                 mail CDATA #IMPLIED
                 title CDATA #IMPLIED>
]>
```

Listing 7.27 Elements with a Set of Attributes   *(continues)*

```
<folks>
    <person floor="3rd" dept="pruning" mail="4J" title="anncr">
        <name>Jessica Fenn</name>
        <email>eyes@wig.net</email>
    </person>
    <person>
        <name>Elizabeth Shelly</name>
        <email>lizshell@belugalake.com</email>
    </person>
    <person>
        <name>Mary Franken</name>
        <email>marfran@belugalake.com</email>
    </person>
</folks>
```

Listing 7.27   (*continued*)

```
<?xml version="1.0" standalone="yes"?>
<folks>
    <person floor="3rd" mail="4J">
        <name>
            Jessica Fenn
        </name>
        <email>
            eyes@wig.net
        </email>
    </person>
    <person dept="pruning" mail="4J">
        <name>
            Elizabeth Shelly
        </name>
        <email>
            lizshell@belugalake.com
        </email>
    </person>
    <person dept="pruning" title="anncr">
        <name>
            Mary Franken
        </name>
        <email>
            marfran@belugalake.com
        </email>
    </person>
</folks>
```

Listing 7.28   The Result of Copying and Moving Attributes

> **NOTE** There is a method named `setAttributeNode()` that is defined as part of the `Element` interface. This method should allow you to attach a complete `Attr` object to an `Element`, but the method did not work properly in the version of JAXP used to develop the example programs for this book, so no example has been included. When a working version of the method is released, an example will be posted to the Web site of this book.

Locating a Node by an ID

It's possible to use the DTD to designate one of the attributes as the ID specifier for a node. This ID can then be used to locate the node. It is the same idea as specifying some field in the record of a database as being the key and then using the individual key values to locate the records.

An `Element` node can have one, and only one, of its attribute names designated as its ID. For an attribute to be used as an ID, it must be declared as such in the DTD, as shown in the example in Listing 7.29. Whenever a search is made for the ID value, the name of the attribute is not involved; it's the value of the attribute that's used to locate the `Element` node This means that the attribute value must be unique for the entire document, even if different elements are defined with ID attributes of different names. If there are duplicate attribute values, a search will find one of them, but there is no way to know ahead of time which one it will be.

As shown in Listing 7.29, the ID named `nick` is defined as an attribute of the `"name"` element. The XML contains three `"name"` elements, each of which contains its

```
<?xml version="1.0" standalone="yes"?>
<!DOCTYPE folks [
<!ELEMENT folks (person)*>
<!ELEMENT person (name)>
<!ELEMENT name (#PCDATA)>
<!ATTLIST name nick ID #IMPLIED>
]>

<folks>
    <person>
        <name nick="Al">Alite Quandry</name>
    </person>
    <person>
        <name nick="Fred">Mush Pushkin</name>
    </person>
    <person>
        <name nick="Alvie">Avarine Spraddle</name>
    </person>
</folks>
```

Listing 7.29 An XML Document with ID Tags on Names

```
public void findByID(Document doc,String idName) {
    Element name = doc.getElementById(idName);
    if (name == null) {
        System.out.println("There is no element with the ID "
                + idName);
    } else {
        Text text = (Text)name.getFirstChild();
        System.out.println("The ID " + idName
                + " locates the name " + text.getData());
    }
}
```

Listing 7.30   A Method to Find an ID Value and Print the Element Text

```
The ID Alvie locates the name Avarine Spraddle
The ID Fred locates the name Mush Pushkin
There is no element with the ID Migs
The ID Al locates the name Alite Quandry
```

Listing 7.31   The Result of Four ID Lookups

own ID identifier. The method shown in Listing 7.30 searches the entire document tree, beginning from the root, to find a specific ID value and, if it finds one, it lists the text it finds at that location. If the search returns `null`, there is no `Element` of any kind in the entire document that has that particular ID value.

Using Listing 7.29 as the document to build the parse tree, and calling the method in Listing 7.30 four times with the strings "Alvie", "Fred", "Migs", and "Al", the output looks like that in Listing 7.31.

Editing the Text of a Node

There is more than one way to change the text of a `Text` node. You can replace the entire `Text` node or you can replace only the `Text` inside the node. There are also some methods that you can use to directly edit the character strings stored in a `Text` node. In fact, because these editing methods are defined as part of the `CharacterData` interface, the same editing techniques can be applied to `CDATASection` and `Comment` nodes because they both extend the `CharacterData` interface. The editing examples in this section demonstrate these techniques using the pair of `Text` nodes in the document shown in Listing 7.32.

The first editing technique is to simply replace the character string stored in the `Text` nodes. This is done by the method named `edit1()` shown in Listing 7.33. The first four lines of the method locate the two `Text` nodes that are to have their contents replaced. You

```
<?xml version="1.0" standalone="yes"?>
<!DOCTYPE locations [
<!ELEMENT locations (place)*>
<!ELEMENT place (name | directions)*>
<!ELEMENT name (#PCDATA)>
<!ELEMENT directions (#PCDATA)>
]>

<locations>
    <place>
        <name>Fishing hole</name>
        <directions>Turn left at bridge</directions>
    </place>
</locations>
```

Listing 7.32 A Document with Two Simple `Text` Nodes

can see where double method calls are used to retrieve the child of a child in a single statement. This works, but you must be certain that both the child and grandchild nodes exist
because these methods return `null` if there is no node present, and this could cause your
program to crash. The last two lines of the method call the `setData()` methods of the two
`Text` nodes to replace the existing character strings. The result is shown in Listing 7.34.

There are some methods that enable you to perform substring operations to modify
the existing strings of characters. Of course, you could simply use `getData()` to retrieve the entire string, modify it using Java string operations, and then call `setData()`
to put it back, but there are some methods included with the node that make it possible for your program to edit the text directly. The method named `edit2()` shown in
Listing 7.35 uses the text from the two elements in Listing 7.32 to demonstrate how
editing can be done inside the node.

The method `edit2()` begins by locating the two `Text` nodes and storing their address in the references named `name` and `directions`. The example is kept simple by
assuming that input is exactly as shown in Listing 7.32 and produces the output shown
in Listing 7.36. The word *hole* is deleted from the first line of text by calling the method

```
public void edit1(Document doc) {
    Element root = doc.getDocumentElement();
    Element place = (Element)root.getFirstChild();
    Text name = (Text)place.getFirstChild().getFirstChild();
    Text directions = (Text)place.getLastChild().getFirstChild();

    name.setData("Secret fishing hole");
    directions.setData("Turn left one mile past bridge");
}
```

Listing 7.33 Modifying Text by Replacement

```
<?xml version="1.0" standalone="yes"?>
<locations>
    <place>
        <name>
            Secret fishing hole
        </name>
        <directions>
            Turn left one mile past bridge
        </directions>
    </place>
</locations>
```

Listing 7.34   The Result of Replacing Character Strings

```
public void edit2(Document doc) {
    int length;
    int count;
    int offset;

    Element root = doc.getDocumentElement();
    Element place = (Element)root.getFirstChild();
    Text name = (Text)place.getFirstChild().getFirstChild();
    Text directions = (Text)place.getLastChild().getFirstChild();

    // Delete the word "hole"
    length = name.getLength();
    count = 4;
    offset = length - 4;
    name.deleteData(offset,count);

    // Extract the word "bridge"
    length = directions.getLength();
    count = 6;
    offset = length - count;
    String bridge = directions.substringData(offset,count);

    // Append the word "bridge"
    name.appendData(bridge);

    // Delete " left"
    count = 5;
    offset = 4;
    directions.deleteData(offset,count);
}
```

Listing 7.35   Modifying Text by Cutting and Pasting

```
<?xml version="1.0" standalone="yes"?>
<locations>
    <place>
        <name>
            Fishing bridge
        </name>
        <directions>
            Turn at bridge
        </directions>
    </place>
</locations>
```

Listing 7.36   The Result of Manipulating Strings

deleteData() with the offset to the first character to be deleted and a count of the number of characters to delete. In this example they are the last four characters of the line, but they could have been any characters anywhere in the line. Next, using the same type of offset and count values, the word *bridge* is copied out of the character string of the second line of text with a call to substringData(). The extracted word *bridge* is then added onto the end of the first string with the call to appendData(). Finally, another call is made to deleteData() to remove the word left by removing the five characters beginning at an offset of 4 into the string (the first character of the string being at offset 0).

Along with the appendData() method used in Listing 7.35, there are two other methods that can also be used to add text to an existing string. Listing 7.37 is a method

```
public void edit3(Document doc) {
    int count;
    int offset;

    Element root = doc.getDocumentElement();
    Element place = (Element)root.getFirstChild();
    Text name = (Text)place.getFirstChild().getFirstChild();
    Text directions = (Text)place.getLastChild().getFirstChild();

    // Inserting the word "black"
    offset = 7;
    name.insertData(offset," black");

    // Replace "left" with "right"
    offset = 5;
    count = 4;
    directions.replaceData(offset,count,"right");
}
```

Listing 7.37   Edit Text by Insertion and Replacement

```
<?xml version="1.0" standalone="yes"?>
<locations>
    <place>
        <name>
            Fishing black hole
        </name>
        <directions>
            Turn right at bridge
        </directions>
    </place>
</locations>
```

Listing 7.38   Result of Inserting and Replacing Strings

that demonstrates how to insert text into the middle of a string (always making the string longer) and how to replace existing text with new text (which could make the string either longer or shorter). The results of the edits are shown in Listing 7.38.

Inserting a CDATASection Node

A CDATASection node serves the same purpose as a Text node, except that in a CDATASection the text is preformatted with newline characters, tabs, and whatever other special formatting character you might want to include. Also, like a Text node, it is a very simple process to create a new CDATASection node and insert it into the document.

The input XML is shown in Listing 7.32. It contains a simple text description of some directions to get to a location. The method named addCDATA() shown in Listing 7.39

```
public void addCDATA(Document doc) {
    Element root = doc.getDocumentElement();
    Element place = (Element)root.getFirstChild();
    Element directions = (Element)place.getLastChild();
    String dirtext =
        "Go 9 miles north on highway\n" +
        "Turn left on North Fork road\n" +
        "Turn left after first bridge\n" +
        "At river bend 100 yards from bridge.";
    CDATASection dirdata = doc.createCDATASection(dirtext);
    directions.replaceChild(dirdata,directions.getFirstChild());
}
```

Listing 7.39   A Method for Replacing a Text Node with a New CDATASection Node

```
<?xml version="1.0" standalone="yes"?>
<locations>
    <place>
        <name>
            Fishing hole
        </name>
        <directions>
            <![CDATA[Go 9 miles north on highway
Turn left on North Fork road
Turn left after first bridge
At river bend 100 yards from bridge.]]>
        </directions>
    </place>
</locations>
```

Listing 7.40 An XML Document with a CDATA Section

edits the parse tree by replacing the simple Text node with a CDATASection node containing formatted text. The resulting form of the XML is shown in Listing 7.40.

The first three lines of the method in Listing 7.39 locate the directions Element node in the parse tree. The String object named dirtext is constructed to include some special characters; in Listing 7.39 there are three newline characters used to break the text, so there is only one step described on each line of the formatted directions text in Listing 7.40. A new CDATASection node is created by calling the method create-CDATASection() that is found in the Document object. This is a convenience method that can be used to get new CDATASection objects to be placed at any location in the parse tree. The last line of the method, the call to replaceChild(), inserts the new CDATASection node in place of the existing Text node.

Splitting a Text Node

It's possible to split a single Text node into two Text nodes. By specifying an offset into the text, you control how much of the text remains in the original node and how much is moved to the new node. If the node being split has a parent, the new node is inserted as the next sibling following the original node and becomes a new child node of the same parent. The result is that the text is in the same order as it was before, but it's now spread across two nodes.

The example document in Listing 7.41 contains an element that, when parsed into a DOM tree, creates a single Text node with one block of text. This text could actually be much longer than the one shown; it's not uncommon for a document to be composed of several large paragraphs and to have many of the paragraphs exist as a single line of text. For this small example, the method shown in Listing 7.42 breaks the Text node into three separate nodes, resulting in three Text nodes existing as siblings as shown in Listing 7.43.

The split() method in Listing 7.42 locates the original Text node and splits it into two pieces by calling splitText() with an offset of 20. This results in the original node retaining only the first 20 characters of the text, with the remaining characters being used to create a new node. Two things happen with this new node: It is added to the parse tree as a sibling to the original node, and it is returned from the split() method call. The last line of the split() method then calls splitText() with an offset of 50 for the newly created node, causing the node to split again and resulting in there being three Text nodes produced from the original one. Writing this new parse tree to an XML file results in something that looks like Listing 7.43.

```
<?xml version="1.0" standalone="yes"?>
<!DOCTYPE story [
<!ELEMENT story (paragraph)*>
<!ELEMENT paragraph (#PCDATA)>
]>

<story>
    <paragraph>Once upon a time there was a large fishing hole. In this
hole there was known to be a really big fish.</paragraph>
</story>
```

Listing 7.41   An Element with a Single Block of Text

```
public void split(Document doc) {

    Element root = doc.getDocumentElement();
    Element paragraph = (Element)root.getFirstChild();
    Text text = (Text)paragraph.getFirstChild();
    Text newText = text.splitText(20);
    newText.splitText(50);
}
```

Listing 7.42   Splitting One Text Node into Three

```
<?xml version="1.0" standalone="yes"?>
<story>
    <paragraph>
        Once upon a time the
        re was a large fishing hole. In this hole there wa
        s known to be a really big fish.
    </paragraph>
</story>
```

Listing 7.43   Three Text Nodes in One Element

```
    public void normalize(Document doc) {
        Element root = doc.getDocumentElement();
        root.normalize();
    }
}
```

Listing 7.44 Normalize All of the Text in a Document

The split text form shown in Listing 7.43 is not quite right for an XML document because parsing this document into a tree wouldn't result in three Text nodes because it's a continuous block of text without any intervening elements. The best approach is to clean things up while the document is still in the form of a parse tree. In a complicated document, any number of edits could have added and removed blocks of text, and even entire subtrees of document and document markups could have been combined in all sorts of ways. This process could leave a parse tree in such a condition that there could be any number of blocks of text that are adjacent to one another and should be combined into a more normalized tree. This cleanup process could be a tedious task, but there is a method named normalize() that you can call that will scan a document tree and clean up the text. The method shown in Listing 7.44 calls the normalize() method of the root element of the tree, which will cause an examination of the entire tree, and any Text nodes that need cleaning up will be combined properly. CDATASection nodes aren't processed this way because of the special characters they contain, so you'll need to take care of those yourself.

Creating a Parse Tree from Scratch

It's possible to construct a parse tree from scratch without first parsing an XML document. This would be your approach if you wanted to create a completely new document in your application. The class DOMNew shown in Listing 7.45 creates a new tree, adds some elements to it, and then uses a TreeToXML object to output the result as shown in Listing 7.46.

To create a new Document the process begins the same way as it would if the parser were going to be used to read an XML document. A DocumentBuilderFactory is configured and used to acquire a DocumentBuilder. Instead of using the DocumentBuilder to parse input, the newDocument() method is called to create a new (and empty) Document object. In this example, the buildTree() method is then called to populate the parse tree.

The buildTree() method begins by creating and inserting the root node. In this example it is a "places" element, and it has two child nodes, each of which is the name of a place. The resulting document is shown as XML in Listing 7.46.

```java
import javax.xml.parsers.DocumentBuilder;
import javax.xml.parsers.DocumentBuilderFactory;
import org.w3c.dom.Document;
import org.w3c.dom.Element;
import org.w3c.dom.Text;
import javax.xml.parsers.ParserConfigurationException;
import java.io.*;

public class DOMNew {
    static public void main(String[] arg) {
        if(arg.length != 1) {
            System.err.println("Usage: DOMNew <outfile>");
            System.exit(1);
        }
        DOMNew dc = new DOMNew();
        dc.createNew(arg[0]);
    }
    public void createNew(String outfile) {
        DocumentBuilderFactory dbf =
DocumentBuilderFactory.newInstance();
        dbf.setValidating(true);
        dbf.setNamespaceAware(true);
        dbf.setIgnoringElementContentWhitespace(true);

        Document doc = null;
        try {
            DocumentBuilder builder = dbf.newDocumentBuilder();
            doc = builder.newDocument();
            buildTree(doc);
            FileOutputStream fos = new FileOutputStream(outfile);
            TreeToXML ttxml = new TreeToXML();
            ttxml.write(fos,doc);
            fos.close();
        } catch (ParserConfigurationException e) {
            System.err.println(e);
            System.exit(1);
        } catch (IOException e) {
            System.err.println(e);
            System.exit(1);
        }
    }
    public void buildTree(Document doc) {
        Element name;
        Text text;
        Element root = doc.createElement("places");
        doc.appendChild(root);
        name = doc.createElement("name");
        text = doc.createTextNode("Algonquin Roundtable");
        name.appendChild(text);
        root.appendChild(name);
        name = doc.createElement("name");
        text = doc.createTextNode("Bayou Teche");
        name.appendChild(text);
        root.appendChild(name);
    }
}
```

Listing 7.45 A Class That Creates a New DOM Parse Tree

```
<?xml version="1.0"?>
<places>
    <name>
        Algonquin Roundtable
    </name>
    <name>
        Bayou Teche
    </name>
</places>
```

Listing 7.46   An XML Document Constructed from Scratch

Moving Nodes between Documents

It's possible to have two (or even more) document parse trees loaded into memory simultaneously, and you can cut and paste things between them, but some things must be taken into consideration when you do this. For one thing, the documents could have been based on different DTDs and could contain a completely different set of element names. Also, the parser and document factory that produced each one could have used a different set of configuration settings, causing some subtle (and some not so subtle) differences in the internal format of the parse tree. To overcome these problems, there's a set of special API members that will *import* an external node into the current tree by making all the necessary internal conversions. This conversion technique can be applied to the importation of a single node or to several nodes simultaneously in the form of a subtree. All you do is import a single node, and if it has any child nodes, they will be imported also.

The class in Listing 7.47 loads two separate documents into parse trees and then makes a duplicate of a subtree from one of them and attaches it to the other tree.

A Document object (root of the parse trees) is constructed for each of the two XML documents. The one named doc1 is the parse tree of the document shown in Listing 7.48 and doc2 is the tree for the document in Listing 7.49. For convenience the same DocumentBuilder is used to construct both parse trees, but the actions and results would be the same if two different DocumentBuilders had been used.

The method importName() in Listing 7.47 extracts an entry from doc1 and copies it into doc2. Once the node to be copied is selected (in this case, the one named personInDoc1), a call is made to importNode() of the target parse tree to create a copy of the original tree node. The importNode() method makes a duplicate of the original node and changes it as necessary to fit the configuration of the target tree. The second argument to importNode() has to do with the depth of the copy and is explained in the following paragraphs. The original node is left untouched—only the copy is modified. The Node returned from the call to importNode() has no parent, so it is necessary to make a call to appendChild() to actually insert the new node into

```
import javax.xml.parsers.DocumentBuilder;
import javax.xml.parsers.DocumentBuilderFactory;
import org.w3c.dom.Document;
import org.w3c.dom.Node;
import org.w3c.dom.Element;
import org.xml.sax.InputSource;
import org.xml.sax.SAXException;
import javax.xml.parsers.ParserConfigurationException;
import java.io.*;

public class DOMImport {
    static public void main(String[] arg) {
        if(arg.length != 3) {
            System.err.println(
                    "Usage: DOMImport <infile1> <infile2> <outfile>");
            System.exit(1);
        }
        DOMImport dc = new DOMImport();
        dc.inandout(arg[0],arg[1],arg[2]);
    }
    public void inandout(String infile1,String infile2,String outfile) {
        DocumentBuilderFactory dbf =
DocumentBuilderFactory.newInstance();
        dbf.setValidating(true);
        dbf.setNamespaceAware(true);
        dbf.setIgnoringElementContentWhitespace(true);

        Document doc1 = null;
        Document doc2 = null;
        try {
            DocumentBuilder builder = dbf.newDocumentBuilder();
            builder.setErrorHandler(new MyErrorHandler());
            InputSource is1 = new InputSource(infile1);
            doc1 = builder.parse(is1);
            InputSource is2 = new InputSource(infile2);
            doc2 = builder.parse(is2);
            importName(doc1,doc2);
            FileOutputStream fos = new FileOutputStream(outfile);
            TreeToXML ttxml = new TreeToXML();
            ttxml.write(fos,doc2);
            fos.close();
        } catch (SAXException e) {
            System.exit(1);
        } catch (ParserConfigurationException e) {
            System.err.println(e);
            System.exit(1);
        } catch (IOException e) {
            System.err.println(e);
            System.exit(1);
        }
```

Listing 7.47   Copy a Node from One Parse Tree into Another   (*continues*)

```
        }
    public void importName(Document doc1,Document doc2) {
        Element root1 = doc1.getDocumentElement();
        Element personInDoc1 = (Element)root1.getFirstChild();

        Node importedPerson = doc2.importNode(personInDoc1,true);

        Element root2 = doc2.getDocumentElement();
        root2.appendChild(importedPerson);
    }
}
```

Listing 7.47   (*continued*)

```
<?xml version="1.0" standalone="yes"?>
<!DOCTYPE contacts [
<!ELEMENT contacts (person)*>
<!ELEMENT person (name, email)>
<!ELEMENT name (#PCDATA | bold)*>
<!ELEMENT email (#PCDATA)>
]>

<contacts>
    <person>
        <name>Ichobad Crane</name>
        <email>sleepy@hollow.net</email>
    </person>
</contacts>
```

Listing 7.48   An XML Document Providing an Element for Export

```
<?xml version="1.0" standalone="yes"?>
<!DOCTYPE folks [
<!ELEMENT folks (person)*>
<!ELEMENT person (name, phone, email)>
<!ELEMENT name (#PCDATA | bold)*>
<!ELEMENT phone (#PCDATA)>
<!ELEMENT email (#PCDATA)>
]>

<folks>
    <person>
        <name>Zaphod Beeblebrox</name>
        <phone>907 555-9882</phone>
        <email>outer@space.net</email>
    </person>
</folks>
```

Listing 7.49   An XML Document to Receive an Imported Element

```
<?xml version="1.0" standalone="yes"?>
<folks>
    <person>
        <name>
            Zaphod Beeblebrox
        </name>
        <phone>
            907 555-9882
        </phone>
        <email>
            outer@space.net
        </email>
    </person>
    <person>
        <name>
            Ichobad Crane
        </name>
        <email>
            sleepy@hollow.net
        </email>
    </person>
</folks>
```

Listing 7.50   The Result of Inserting the New Node

the tree. The new parse tree resulting from the call to importName() is shown in Listing 7.50.

You may have noticed that the dictionaries of the two XML documents are not the same and, in fact, the new entry inserted into the parse tree of the second document actually violates the dictionary definitions of the original document. This situation is true not just for imported nodes, but for all parse trees. There's no checking against the original document's dictionary, so it's quite easy to produce parse trees that couldn't be parsed from an actual document because of these violations. It's up to the application to make sure the edits made to the parse tree are valid and have meaning when they're output.

There are two arguments passed to the importNode() method. The first one is the node to be duplicated and the second one is true if the copy is to be deep and false if it is to be shallow. The exact meaning of deep and shallow will vary a bit depending on the type of node, so there's an explanation of the actions for each node type listed in Table 7.1. For some types of nodes the deep parameter on the importNode() method has a special meaning, but for others it has no effect.

Table 7.1 Results of Calling importNode() for Different Node Types

NODE TYPE	ACTION
ATTRIBUTE_NODE	Setting the deep parameter has no effect because a deep copy is always made and all child nodes are duplicated into a new subtree. Even if, in the original, the attribute was allowed to default, in the copy the flag is set to true, indicating the attribute has been specified.
CDATA_SECTION_NODE	The node and its values are always duplicated.
COMMENT_NODE	The node and its values are always duplicated.
DOCUMENT_FRAGMENT_NODE	If the deep parameter is set to true, the entire subtree is duplicated. If it is not set to true, the result is an empty DocumentFragment object.
DOCUMENT_NODE	Error. A Document node cannot be imported.
DOCUMENT_TYPE_NODE	Error. A DocumentType node cannot be imported.
ELEMENT_NODE	Any attributes that were specifically included with the element are imported. Default attributes, unless they were actually specified, are not imported (but instead are allowed to default according to the default definitions of the new DTD). Only if the deep parameter is set to true will the nodes of the subtree of the element be imported, and this importation will continue recursively for the entire subtree.
ENTITY_NODE	Although it is possible call importNode() with a node of this type and generate a copy, it is not possible to add it to another parse tree because the DocumentType node cannot be edited in this version of JAXP. The publicId and systemId attributes are copied. If the deep parameter is set, the importation will continue recursively for the entire subtree.
ENTITY_REFERENCE_NODE	The deep parameter has no effect because the source and destination documents may have defined the entity differently. The entity will only have a value if the recipient document has defined the entity.
NOTATION_NODE	Although it is possible call importNode() with a node of this type and generate a copy, it is not possible to add it to the parse tree because the DocumentType node cannot be edited in this version of JAXP. The publicId and systemId attributes are copied.
PROCESSING_INSTRUCTION_NODE	The node and its values are duplicated.
TEXT_NODE	The node and its values are duplicated.

Editing by Using a Document Fragment

As a convenience, when editing a parse tree, it's possible to construct a completely separate subtree and then insert it into the parse tree at a later time. This procedure is not necessary for building a parse tree, but it can be convenient for organizing your program to allow you to write separate modules that create portions of a complete tree.

The example program in Listing 7.51 demonstrates the mechanics of using document fragments. The addFragment() method creates a new DocumentFragment node by calling createDocumentFragment(). A pair of calls are made to makePersonNode() to create a two new "person" nodes, and each of these nodes is attached to the existing root node with calls to appendChild(). A parse tree of the document shown in Listing 7.52 will have new elements added, as shown in Listing 7.53.

The method named makePersonNode() in Listing 7.51 creates a "person" node that contains one "name" node and one "phone" node and then returns the "person" node to the caller. In the addFragment() method a call is made to createDocumentFragment() to create an unattached node that (because of its configuration settings) can be attached as a child to any of the nodes in the Document. The Element nodes returned from calls to makePersonNode() are appended as children

```
public void addFragment(Document doc) {
    Element person;
    Element root = doc.getDocumentElement();
    DocumentFragment fragment = doc.createDocumentFragment();
    person = makePersonNode(doc,"Fred","555-4927");
    fragment.appendChild(person);
    person = makePersonNode(doc,"Sam","555-9832");
    fragment.appendChild(person);
    root.appendChild(fragment);
}
private Element makePersonNode(Document doc,String name,String phone) {
    Element nameNode = doc.createElement("name");
    Text nametextNode = doc.createTextNode(name);
    nameNode.appendChild(nametextNode);

    Element phoneNode = doc.createElement("phone");
    Text phonetextNode = doc.createTextNode(phone);
    phoneNode.appendChild(phonetextNode);

    Element personNode = doc.createElement("person");
    personNode.appendChild(nameNode);
    personNode.appendChild(phoneNode);
    return(personNode);
}
}
```

Listing 7.51   Creating a DocumentFragment Subtree and Appending to the Document

```
<?xml version="1.0" standalone="yes"?>
<!DOCTYPE folks [
<!ELEMENT folks (person)*>
<!ELEMENT person (name, phone)>
<!ELEMENT name (#PCDATA | bold)*>
<!ELEMENT phone (#PCDATA)>
]>

<folks>
    <person>
        <name>Frank Fangston</name>
        <phone>555-3247</phone>
    </person>
</folks>
```

Listing 7.52   A Document Containing a Single Person Node

```
<?xml version="1.0" standalone="yes"?>
<folks>
    <person>
        <name>
            Frank Fangston
        </name>
        <phone>
            555-3247
        </phone>
    </person>
    <person>
        <name>
            Fred
        </name>
        <phone>
            555-4927
        </phone>
    </person>
    <person>
        <name>
            Sam
        </name>
        <phone>
            555-9832
        </phone>
    </person>
</folks>
```

Listing 7.53   A Document Edited by Using a Document Fragment

to the DocumentFragment node. Once the entire document fragment subtree has been constructed, it's appended as a child to an element of the original document tree.

When a DocumentFragment is appended as a child node, the DocumentFragment node itself is not involved. Instead, each of the child nodes of the Document-Fragment is appended, but the DocumentFragment node itself is discarded. The only purpose of the DocumentFragment node was to act as the root node during the construction of the subtree, and once that is done, it's no longer needed.

Inserting a Processing Instruction and Comment

It's a simple matter to insert either a processing instruction or a comment into the parse tree. The methods shown in Listing 7.54 insert one of each. Using the example document shown in Listing 7.52 to generate the parse tree, the result of calling the addComment() method and then the addProcessingInstruction() method is shown in Listing 7.55.

Both the comment and the processing instruction tree nodes are created by calls to methods in the Document node of the parse tree. In the addComment() method of Listing 7.54 a call to createComment() is made to create a new Comment node. In the addProcessingInstruction() method a call to createProcessing-Instruction() method uses the two strings passed to it to create the node. The first string is the name of the processing instruction and the second is the entire body of the instruction. In this example, for the body of the process instruction, the standard form of a name being assigned a value is used, but a processing instruction string can actually take any form you would like; it just needs to be understood by the process reading the information.

```
public void addComment(Document doc) {
    Element root = doc.getDocumentElement();
    Element folks = (Element)root.getLastChild();
    Comment comment = doc.createComment("Text of the comment");
    root.insertBefore(comment,folks);
}
public void addProcessingInstruction(Document doc) {
    Element root = doc.getDocumentElement();
    Element folks = (Element)root.getLastChild();
    ProcessingInstruction pi;
    pi = (ProcessingInstruction)doc.createProcessingInstruction(
        "validate",
        "phone=\"lookup\"");
    root.insertBefore(pi,folks);
}
```

Listing 7.54   Methods to Insert a Processing Instruction and a Comment

```
<?xml version="1.0" standalone="yes"?>
<folks>
    <!-- Text of the comment -->
    <?validate phone="lookup"?>
    <person>
        <name>
            Frank Fangston
        </name>
        <phone>
            555-3247
        </phone>
    </person>
</folks>
```

Listing 7.55   The Addition of a Comment and a Processing Instruction

Summary

This chapter has explored the details of constructing and manipulating a DOM parse tree. Examples demonstrated methods for pruning the tree by removing and adding nodes. It is even possible to move nodes from one location to another, even if the locations are in separate parse trees. Text can be modified by deleting nodes from the tree and inserting a new node, with the modified text, in its place. Alternatively, the text can be edited inside a tree node by using some cut and paste methods designed for that task.

The next chapter is also about editing XML documents, but in an entirely different way. It shows how to use XSL to write a set of editing rules, apply them to the tree form of a document, and then output the results of the edit. This process is known as *transformation*.

CHAPTER

8

JAXP XSL Document Transformations

Translating an XML document into another form, such as a database record or HTML document, is possible by reading the document with SAX or DOM and writing Java code to produce the output. But there is another approach. In most cases the same goal can be achieved by writing Extensible Stylesheet Language (XSL) instead of using Java classes and methods. Applying an XSL stylesheet to an XML document is known as a *transforming* a document.

The vocabulary of commands that are used inside XSL to apply a transformation is quite large. This chapter presents the basic set of commands and demonstrates how they can be used to transform a document. When you write your XSL transformations according to the contents of the DTD that is used to create the XML input documents, the transformation process will work with any input document that adheres to that DTD. Thus no matter what the source of the XML document, as long as it is created according to the constraints of the DTD, it can be successfully transformed by the XSL document designed for it. In fact, if you want to have optional ways of formatting the display, you can write a whole family of XSL transformation documents using whichever one you would like to format the XML for display.

During the transformation process, XSL may need to rearrange the data found in the input XML document. This is achieved by loading the document into a parse tree and then moving from one node to another as the output is created. The expressions used to specify these moves from one node to another are known as *XPath expressions*. An

XPath expression specifies the location of the starting point of a search, the destination (target) of the search, and possibly the path to follow to find the target.

Once the XPath expression has been located, the instructions that are applied to create the output are a collection of one or more XML Transformation, or *XSLT,* () elements. The XSLT elements, or commands, make up a language that you can use to specify what data from a node is to be output, and how it is to be output. There are many commands that can be used to produce output. This chapter describes the most fundamental commands and provides examples of their use. In fact, the information presented in this chapter is all you will need to create most Web pages.

Performing a Transformation

When the facilities of JAXP are used, the Java portion of actually performing a transformation is quite simple. The transformation processor is built into JAXP, so all you have to do is provide it with an XML document to be transformed, an XSL document to control the transformation, and the name of an output file. Actually, the two inputs and the one output are all Java streams, so they can come from and go to anyplace that Java is capable of reading and writing stream data. For example, the input could come from an XML server that extracted the data from a database, the XSL document could be a local file stored on disk, and the output could be a Web page file stored somewhere in the publicly accessible directories of a Web server. In fact, inside a Java-based Web server, the transformation process could have been started as the result of a request made by a remote Web browser, and the output could be streamed, in HTML format, directly across an HTTP link to the requesting browser.

The program in Listing 8.1 accepts three file names (two input and one output) on the command line and performs a transformation. The static method `newInstance()` of the `TransformerFactory` class is called to return an instance of a `Transformer-Factory`. The factory method `newTransformer()` is then supplied with an XSL input stream so that it can create a `Transformer` object. The `Transformer` object does the actual transforming. It reads the set of instruction templates found in the XSL document and is ready to perform transformations. The program shown in Listing 8.1 only performs one transformation and then stops, but it is possible to use the same `Transformer` object to perform any number of transformations, as long as they are all based on the same XSL transformation document. The transformation takes place in the last line of the class where there is a call to the `transform()` method of the `Trans-fomer` object. This one method does the actual work of converting the data from the input stream and sending it to the output stream.

In the `SimpleTransform` program of Listing 8.1, a new `Transformer` object is created and its `setErrorListener()` method is called with a new `ErrorListener` object. The `ErrorListener` interface is very similar to the `ErrorHandler` that was introduced in Chapter 4; however, the `ErrorListener` not only will be required to process the input and parser errors of the `ErrorHandler`, but it will also receive any error conditions that appear in the XSL document or any that may occur during the transformation process. That is, the input document may parse perfectly into a tree, but

```
import javax.xml.transform.TransformerFactory;
import javax.xml.transform.Transformer;
import javax.xml.transform.stream.StreamSource;
import javax.xml.transform.stream.StreamResult;

import javax.xml.transform.TransformerConfigurationException;
import javax.xml.transform.TransformerException;

public class SimpleTransform {
    static public void main(String[] arg) {
        if(arg.length != 3) {
            System.err.println("Usage: SimpleTransform " +
                "<input.xml> <input.xsl> <output>");
            System.exit(1);
        }
        String inXML = arg[0];
        String inXSL = arg[1];
        String outTXT = arg[2];

        SimpleTransform st = new SimpleTransform();
        try {
            st.transform(inXML,inXSL,outTXT);
        } catch(TransformerConfigurationException e) {
            System.err.println("Invalid factory configuration");
            System.err.println(e);
        } catch(TransformerException e) {
            System.err.println("Error during transformation");
            System.err.println(e);
        }
    }
    public void transform(String inXML,String inXSL,String outTXT)
                throws TransformerConfigurationException,
                    TransformerException {

        TransformerFactory factory = TransformerFactory.newInstance();

        StreamSource xslStream = new StreamSource(inXSL);
        Transformer transformer = factory.newTransformer(xslStream);
        transformer.setErrorListener(new MyErrorListener());

        StreamSource in = new StreamSource(inXML);
        StreamResult out = new StreamResult(outTXT);
        transformer.transform(in,out);
    }
}
```

Listing 8.1   A Program That Performs XML Transformations

```
import javax.xml.transform.ErrorListener;
import javax.xml.transform.TransformerException;

public class MyErrorListener implements ErrorListener {
    public void warning(TransformerException e)
                throws TransformerException {
        show("Warning",e);
        throw(e);
    }
    public void error(TransformerException e)
                throws TransformerException {
        show("Error",e);
        throw(e);
    }
    public void fatalError(TransformerException e)
                throws TransformerException {
        show("Fatal Error",e);
        throw(e);
    }
    private void show(String type,TransformerException e) {
        System.out.println(type + ": " + e.getMessage());
        if(e.getLocationAsString() != null)
            System.out.println(e.getLocationAsString());
    }
}
```

Listing 8.2   An Error Listener Processes Error Messages from a Transformation

it could still clash with something during the conversion process. Listing 8.2 is an implementation of the ErrorListener interface that defines the same action for all three levels of error; it simply reports the error and throws the exception that was passed to it. It's up to you to decide how your application is to react, but it is possible to ignore messages passed to the warning() method and even those passed to the error() method. When the fatal() method is called, however, generally any attempt to continue the transformation process would be futile. In Listing 8.2, the Transformer-Exception objects are used as the argument to a show() method to display the error condition, and the exception is then thrown. This action is fine for a simple demonstration program such as this, but if you are installing an XSL transformer into a production system, you will need to do something a bit more robust. The way the errors are handled here, the exceptional condition may never be noticed by the user if the process is being run other than from the command line.

```
<?xml version="1.0"?>
<xsl:stylesheet
        xmlns:xsl="http://www.w3.org/1999/XSL/Transform"
        version="1.0">
  <xsl:template match="/">
    Ignore the input and output this line.
  </xsl:template>
</xsl:stylesheet>
```

Listing 8.3   The Basic Form of an XSL Stylesheet Document

Listing 8.3 contains an XSL document that generates very simple output. You can use any XML document you wish as input, and the output will be the same because this XSL document completely ignores the input and generates one line of output.

The stylesheet in Listing 8.3 contains all of the required pieces of an XSL document. As you can see, this document is an XML document right down to the declaration line at the very top. All of the XSL elements and commands are in the xsl namespace, so the namespace is declared by xmlns in the root element (which is always named xsl:stylesheet). Recall from Chapter 2 that the URI specified on the xmlns namespace definition does not contain any defining information. It is only used as a unique string to differentiate it from any other namespaces you may want use in the document. The version number is an attribute of the xsl:stylesheet element and is required. It must be present to specify the version number of the XML document to be transformed.

If the input document you are going to be transforming contains namespaces, you will need to declare them along with your xsl namespace declaration. For example, if your input document were to use the namespaces tally and maglist, your root declaration would need to be laid out something like the following:

```
<xsl:stylesheet
        xmlns:xsl="http://www.w3.org/1999/XSL/Transform"
        xmlns:tally="http://www.belugalake.com/showtally"
        xmlns:maglist="http://www.wiley.com/javaxml/magma"
        version="1.0">
```

The rest of the stylesheet is made up of a set of predefined top-level xsl elements. Most of these are xsl:template elements because it is these templates that do the actual transformation, and a useful XSL document will normally have a number of templates. All templates have, as a minimum, an expression that matches a node of the input tree and one or more instructions that determine the output. In this example the match attribute uses the simple XPath expression "/" to locate the root node of the input parse tree. The input data is ignored, however, because the only output instruction in the body of the template specifies a static line of text as the output. The output from transforming any XML document will look like the following:

```
<?xml version="1.0" encoding="UTF-8"?>

    Ignore the input and output this line.
```

The output includes an XML header. Actually, although it is usually suppressed when HTML is produced, this header is correct for, and often appears in, an XHTML file. An XHTML file is HTML that is also compliant with the XML syntax for opening and closing element tags. The only other output is the line of text that was in the body of the template because there is no specific instruction to output anything else—there is no default output.

Pattern Matching with XPath

The first requirement for being able to generate output from an XML parse tree is to be able to traverse the tree to locate the nodes. This is done by pattern matching using a language named XPath. Just as the PATH environment variable locates things entered from the command line, an XPath expression can be used to locate a particular node, or a collection of nodes, in the parse tree. The structure of the parse tree traversed by XPath is the same as the DOM parse tree discussed in Chapters 6 and 7. An XPath expression has the following three basic parts:

1. Every path has a starting point. The path may begin at the current node, the root node, or with the parent, child, or sibling of the current node.

2. A path will sometimes have a route to be followed. The route may be as simple as moving to a companion node, or it could be as complicated as the traversal through several named and/or relative nodes in the tree. The route will be nonexistent if the destination is the same as the starting point or if the movement is based on a search.

3. Every path has a destination. In fact, there may be a number of destinations because it is a fairly simple matter to write an XPath expression that matches more than one node.

The basic syntax of an XPath expression is a follows:

```
[axisname::]nodetest[expression1][expression2] ...
```

Every part of the XPath expression is optional except for `nodetest`. The `nodetest` specifies both the path and destination and can be further refined by the expressions that follow it. The expressions are also in the form `axisname::nodetest` and are used to refine the search further. The `axisname` defines the starting point and the initial direction of the path. The default axisname is the current tree node, and the default direction is down the tree to the nodes below. As shown in Table 8.1 the child axis name is specified as the default. The nodetest is usually the name of the destination node but, as shown in Table 8.2, there are some other expressions that can be used in its place.

As you can see from the lists in Tables 8.1 and 8.2, a lot of options are available. More than that, it is possible to use a combination of any number of these options in a single

Table 8.1 The Defined Axis Names of an XPath Expression

AXIS NAME	DESCRIPTION
child	The children of the current node. This is the default used if no axis is specified.
descendant	All of the children, grandchildren, and so on, of the current node.
parent	The node that is the parent of the current node.
ancestor	All of the parents, grandparents, and so on, of the current node to the root of the tree.
following	All nodes created from elements that came after the element of the current node in the input document.
preceding	All nodes created from elements that came before the element of the current node in the input document.
following-sibling	All of the parse tree siblings of the current node that come after the current node.
preceding-sibling	All of the parse tree siblings of the current node that come before the current node.
attribute	The attribute nodes of the current node.
@	A short form of attribute.
namespace	The namespace node of the current node.
self	The current node.
descendent-or-self	The current node and all of the children, grandchildren, and so on.
ancestor-or-self	The current node, its parents, grandparents, and so on to the root of the tree.

Table 8.2   The Node Tests for Specifying the Destination of an XPath Expression

PATTERN	DEFINITION
/	Matches the root node
*	Matches any node
name	Matches nodes for an element named "name"
name1 | name2	Matches nodes for elements named either "name1" or "name2"
name1 / name2	Matches nodes for elements named "name1" with a parent element named "name2"
name1 // name2	Matches nodes for elements named "name2" with a child element named "name1"
.	Matches the current node
..	Matches the parent of the current node
text()	Matches any text node
comment()	Matches any comment node
id(name)	Matches any node with an ID attribute value of "name"
processing-instruction()	Matches any processing instruction node
node()	Matches any node type
position()=n	Matches the nth occurrence in the list of previously matched nodes
last()	Returns the number of nodes matched

Table 8.3   Examples of XPath Expressions

XPATH	DESCRIPTION
child::person	All the nodes named "person" beneath the current node.
person	The same as child::person because the axis name child is the default.
child::/	The root node. The axis name doesn't matter because the slash character always addresses the root.
/	The same as child::/ because the axis name child is the default.

Table 8.3 *(continued)*

XPATH	DESCRIPTION
`child::person[position()=1]`	The first node in a list of person nodes.
`person[1]`	The same as child::person[position()=1] because child is assumed and a number is assumed to be a position.
`child::person[position()=last()]`	The last node in a list of person nodes.
`child::person[last()]/child::name`	The name node of the last person node.
`person[position()=2]/name`	The name node of the second person node.
`person[attribute::id="p324"]`	The person node with an ID attribute value of "p324".
`person[@manager]`	A person node with a manager attribute set.
`parent::*`	The parent of the current node.
`parent::person`	The parent node, but only if it is named person.
`next-sibling::phone`	The sibling node named phone.

XPath definition. Table 8.3 lists some of the more common forms, and it also contains some examples to demonstrate how combinations defining more complicated paths can be constructed.

XSL Transformations

An XSL stylesheet is an XML document that is written to conform to the XSL DTD. That is, it has a large number of predefined tag names used to create elements that determine the output. The most common output format is HTML, although the actual output can be just about anything you can image. The elements inside the root element are template rules. A template rule is made up of two parts. The first part matches a node in the source tree, and the second one specifies how the node is to be transformed. This basic form allows you to write an XSL stylesheet in such a way that it can be applied to an entire family of input documents. The basic form looks like the following:

```
<xsl:template match="path expression">
    template body
</xsl:template>
```

```
<?xml version="1.0"?>
<xsl:stylesheet
      xmlns:xsl="http://www.w3.org/1999/XSL/Transform"
      version="1.0">
  <xsl:template match="/">
      <xsl:apply-templates/>
  </xsl:template>
</xsl:stylesheet>
```

Listing 8.4   An XSL Stylesheet to Output Unformatted Text

The XSL document in Listing 8.4 will write all of the input text to the output. The element xsl:apply-templates is a command to apply all the other templates to the elements of the input source document. However, in this example there are no other templates, so when this transformation is applied to the XML document shown in Listing 8.5, the output looks like Listing 8.6. Note that although there is no HTML formatting, all of the spaces and newlines are retained in the output. It works this way because, when xsl:apply-templates is executed and there is no template to match an input element, all of the text of that element is sent to the output. This output procedure continues recursively for all input elements that have no matching template.

To move one step up the ladder to improved formatted output, it is possible to add a few HTML tags to make the output document into an HTML page, which can be done by modifying Listing 8.4 to look like Listing 8.7. You will probably recognize the tags for a basic HTML document that are included inside the template as text. Even though they have the opening and closing angle brackets of tags, and would normally

```
<?xml version="1.0" standalone="yes"?>

<folks>
    <person>
        <name>Cugat, Xavier</name>
        <title>Group Leader</title>
        <email>cugie@nosuch.net</email>
        <phone>504 555-8922</phone>
    </person>
    <person>
        <name>Lane, Holly</name>
        <title>Real Estate Agent</title>
        <email>holly@xyz.net</email>
        <phone>314 555-7092</phone>
    </person>
</folks>
```

Listing 8.5   An XML Document Used as Input for Formatting

```
<?xml version="1.0" encoding="UTF-8"?>



        Cugat, Xavier
        Group Leader
        cugie@nosuch.net
        504 555-8922


        Lane, Holly
        Real Estate Agent
        holly@xyz.net
        314 555-7092
```

Listing 8.6   The Default Output, Which Is Unformatted Text

be a part of the XML document that defines the XSL, they are considered data during transformation because they are not defined as being in the xsl namespace.

The output file shown in Listing 8.8 contains something new. The XSL style header is no longer there. The transformation discovered the HTML tags in the body of the template and assumed an HTML document was being output, which meant there was no need for the XSL heading. In its place a META tag was provided that specifies the content type and the character set.

The form of Listing 8.8 is not complete. Although it outputs the text, it does it in a free-form way that will present all of the text as a single block when a Web browser formats it. There are some other things that must be done to present the data in a cleanly

```
<?xml version="1.0"?>
<xsl:stylesheet
        xmlns:xsl="http://www.w3.org/1999/XSL/Transform"
        version="1.0">
  <xsl:template match="/">
    <html>
    <head>
     <title>Contact Information List</title>
    </head>
    <body>
       <xsl:apply-templates/>
    </body>
    </html>
  </xsl:template>
</xsl:stylesheet>
```

Listing 8.7   Adding HTML Tags around the Output Text

```
<html>
<head>
<META http-equiv="Content-Type" content="text/html; charset=UTF-8">
<title>Contact Information List</title>
</head>
<body>


        Cugat, Xavier
        Group Leader
        cugie@nosuch.net
        504 555-8922



        Lane, Holly
        Real Estate Agent
        holly@xyz.net
        314 555-7092


</body>
</html>
```

Listing 8.8   Output Using HTML Tags

readable format. You could use HTML tags to output the text as a list, as blocks of data, in a table, or in any other form you would like.

Stylesheet Elements

A number of template commands exist, all in the form of elements, which can be used to define the format of data. This section demonstrates how some of the more useful ones can be used.

`xsl:apply-templates`

Text can be formatted into a readable Web page by using only the `xsl:apply-templates` element. This element tries to match other templates with the elements of the input documents and, whenever a match is not found, the text of that node and all of its child nodes are sent to the output. Take the simple input document of Listing 8.9. It contains a single `person` element entry, which makes all the element names unique, and simplifies the processing required to format the output.

The XSL stylesheet in Listing 8.10 shows how the `xsl:apply-templates` element can be used in several templates to output formatted data for each of the element types

```
<?xml version="1.0" standalone="yes"?>

<folks>
    <person>
        <name>Lane, Holly</name>
        <title>Real Estate Agent</title>
        <email>holly@xyz.net</email>
        <phone>314 555-7092</phone>
    </person>
</folks>
```

Listing 8.9   A Simple Document Containing Unique Element Names

```
<?xml version="1.0"?>
<xsl:stylesheet
        xmlns:xsl="http://www.w3.org/1999/XSL/Transform"
        version="1.0">

  <xsl:template match="/">
    <html>
    <head>
     <title>Contact Information List</title>
    </head>
    <body>
      <xsl:apply-templates/>
    </body>
    </html>
  </xsl:template>

  <xsl:template match="name">
    <p><b>
      <xsl:apply-templates/>
    </b></p>
  </xsl:template>

  <xsl:template match="title">
    <p>
      <xsl:apply-templates/>
    </p>
  </xsl:template>

  <xsl:template match="email">
    <p>
      <xsl:apply-templates/>
    </p>
  </xsl:template>
```

Listing 8.10   An XSL Document to Perform Simple Formatting   (*continues*)

```
<xsl:template match="phone">
  <p>
    <xsl:apply-templates/>
  </p>
</xsl:template>
</xsl:stylesheet>
```

Listing 8.10 *(continued)*

found in the source. The result isn't very fancy, as shown in Listing 8.11 and Figure 8.1, but it does have some formatting applied to it

Notice in Listing 8.10 that the HTML tags <p> in the XSL all have a terminal tag </p> matching them; this is a requirement of XSL. Constraining the HTML output to include a closing tag for every opening tag causes the resulting HTML to also be syntactically correct for being parsed as XML. This compatibility is what makes the output document XHTML as well as being HTML. This produces a cleaner and more standard form of HTML that can be read and displayed in a much less ambiguous manner by Web browsers.

If you prefer not to include the closing tag in your HTML, you can use a closing slash on the opening tag. The closing slash is ignored by the Web browser but continues to

```
<html>
<head>
<META http-equiv="Content-Type" content="text/html; charset=UTF-8">
<title>Contact Information List</title>
</head>
<body>


<p>
<b>Lane, Holly</b>
</p>

<p>Real Estate Agent</p>

<p>holly@xyz.net</p>

<p>314 555-7092</p>


</body>
</html>
```

Listing 8.11 A Simple XHTML Document Produced by `xsl:apply-templates`

Figure 8.1   The Display Produced from the HTML in Listing 8.11

be correct for XSL. For example, the template used to format the name could have been written this way:

```
<xsl:template match="name">
  <p /><b>
    <xsl:apply-templates/>
  </b>
</xsl:template>
```

The `<b>` tag must have a closing tag so that the HTML presentation software will know exactly what is being included, but the `<p>` tag has no such requirement because it has no contents—the closing tag can be, and usually is, omitted. When the form `<p/>` is translated by JAXP into HTML, it expands the element as a pair of tags in the form `<p></p>` to be compatible with all Web browsers. Many newer Web browsers can handle the more compact form `<p/>`, but this is not universally the case, so JAXP expands it into the original form to guarantee compatibility. Also, even with Web browsers that can read the new form, there is often a problem with the parser separating out the tokens if there is no space in front of the terminating slash. Because of this, you will often see a space inserted, so the tags look like `<p />` instead of simply `<p/>`. In fact, many people have standardized on this form and always insert the space, no matter what the purpose of the document.

Listing 8.11 is the HTML resulting from using the stylesheet in Listing 8.10 on the XML document in Listing 8.9. Each of the elements containing text was located by name and `xsl:apply-templates` was used to output the text surrounded by tags to format the text.

xsl:value-of

The formatting process presented earlier in Listing 8.10 can be simplified by using `xsl:value-of` elements to retrieve the character data from the other XSL elements. This approach is shown in Listing 8.12.

```
<?xml version="1.0"?>
<xsl:stylesheet
        xmlns:xsl="http://www.w3.org/1999/XSL/Transform"
        version="1.0">

  <xsl:template match="/">
    <html>
    <head>
     <title>Contact Information List</title>
    </head>
    <body>
       <xsl:apply-templates/>
    </body>
    </html>
  </xsl:template>

  <xsl:template match="person">
      <p><b>
      <xsl:value-of select="name"/>
      </b></p>
      <p>
      <xsl:value-of select="title"/>
      </p>
      <p>
      <xsl:value-of select="email"/>
      </p>
      <p>
      <xsl:value-of select="phone"/>
      </p>
  </xsl:template>

</xsl:stylesheet>
```

Listing 8.12   Using `xsl:value-of` to Extract the Text of an Element

The `xsl:value-of` element will extract the text of the node that matches the XPath statement on the `select` attribute. Like the `xsl:apply-templates` element, the `xsl:value-of` element will extract and display text of the nodes matched by XPath but, unlike `xsl:apply-templates`, it will not cause other templates to be executed even if they are present in the document. This really doesn't matter for our example because the starting template (the one that matches the root node) applies all templates, which causes the second template to match the `person` node. Inside the `person` node there are four simple nodes that contain only text, so the text is extracted from each node and inserted between the HTML tags for output. The resulting displayed page is identical to the one produced in the previous section and shown in Figure 8.1.

xsl:for-each

An XPath expression can made to match more that one XML element, but the XSL process can only handle one element at a time. For a number of input XML elements to be processed by the same template, they must each be selected, one at a time. To process a collection of nodes, xsl:for-each can be used to create a loop to format each of the matches, one at a time. Illustrating this process is Listing 8.13, which shows the input XML document.

The XML document in Listing 8.13 contains several repetitions of the person element. Some of the advanced matching expressions like those in Table 8.1 could possibly be used to match each one of these nodes individually, but it would be much simpler to set up a loop that matches each one of them, one at a time. If the output for-

```xml
<?xml version="1.0" standalone="yes"?>

<folks>
    <person>
        <name>Baker, Mary</name>
        <title>Counseler</title>
        <email>maryb@belugalake.net</email>
        <phone>502 555-2192</phone>
    </person>
    <person>
        <name>Cugat, Xavier</name>
        <title>Group Leader</title>
        <email>cugie@nosuch.net</email>
        <phone>504 555-8922</phone>
    </person>
    <person>
        <name>Lane, Holly</name>
        <title>Real Estate Agent</title>
        <email>holly@xyz.net</email>
        <phone>314 555-7092</phone>
    </person>
    <person>
        <name>Riley, Lifa</name>
        <title><emph>Leading Edge</emph> Riveter</title>
        <email>lifar@homernet.net</email>
        <phone>907 555-8901</phone>
    </person>
    <person>
        <name>Valee, Rudy</name>
        <title>Singer<option> of songs</option></title>
        <email>rv@belugalake.com</email>
        <phone>314 555-9910</phone>
    </person>
</folks>
```

Listing 8.13   An XML Document Containing Repeated Entries

matting were to require a different action for each one, each one would need to be matched separately by its own template. But because they are all going to be formatted in exactly the same way, a loop is more appropriate than duplicated code. The XSL document in Listing 8.14 contains just such a loop.

In Listing 8.14 there is initially a match, not just a root node of any name but also on the node named `folks`, which is also the root node. This node has a collection of child nodes, each of which is a `person` node. With the `folks` node being the currently selected node, it is possible to iterate through the child nodes using `xsl:for-each` and a `select` attribute with an XPath expression that matches the node names. All of the commands inside the loop will be executed once for each node in the list. The formatted output is displayed in a Web browser as shown in Figure 8.2.

You may have noticed some embedded elements in the source document, named `emph` and `option`, included with the job titles of the last two entries in the list in the XML file shown in Listing 8.13. Until now these tags have been completely ignored because there have been no templates defined to do anything with them. The XSL document shown in Listing 8.15 is a modification of the one in Listing 8.14, adding

```
<?xml version="1.0"?>
<xsl:stylesheet
        xmlns:xsl="http://www.w3.org/1999/XSL/Transform"
        version="1.0">

  <xsl:template match="folks">
    <html>
    <head>
     <title>Contact Information List</title>
    </head>
    <body>
      <xsl:for-each select="person">
        <p /><b>
        <xsl:value-of select="name"/>
        </b>
        <br />
        <xsl:value-of select="title"/>
        <br />
        <xsl:value-of select="email"/>
        <br />
        <xsl:value-of select="phone"/>
      </xsl:for-each>
    </body>
    </html>
  </xsl:template>

</xsl:stylesheet>
```

Listing 8.14   An XSL Document with a Loop to Format a Collection of Nodes

Figure 8.2   The Result of Formatting Similar Nodes Using `xsl:for-each` Looping

templates that define the formats for these two types. Note that the `title` element is no longer formatted using `xsl:value-of` but now uses `xsl:apply-templates` instead. It does so because of the fundamental difference between the two: The first one ignores any embedded elements it may find in the text, whereas the other will search for, and invoke, any matching templates.

The result of applying Listing 8.15 is shown in Figure 8.3. The emph element simply formats the characters as italic, whereas the template matching the `option` element generates no output whatsoever, effectively removing the optional characters.

`xsl:include` and `xsl:import`

An `xsl:include` element can be used to copy another stylesheet document into the current one, just as if you had used an editor to insert its declarations and templates into the current stylesheet. The included templates are processed and treated just as if they had been part of the document including them. A URI string is used to specify the stylesheet to be included, as follows:

```
<xsl:include href="URI string" />
```

An `xsl:import` element can also be used to bring in templates from another stylesheet. The syntax is the same as the `xsl:include` element:

```
<xsl:import href="URI string" />
```

```
<?xml version="1.0"?>
<xsl:stylesheet
        xmlns:xsl="http://www.w3.org/1999/XSL/Transform"
        version="1.0">

  <xsl:template match="folks">
    <html>
    <head>
     <title>Contact Information List</title>
    </head>
    <body>
      <xsl:for-each select="person">
        <p /><b>
        <xsl:value-of select="name"/>
        </b>
        <br />
        <xsl:apply-templates select="title"/>
        <br />
        <xsl:value-of select="email"/>
        <br />
        <xsl:value-of select="phone"/>
      </xsl:for-each>
    </body>
    </html>
  </xsl:template>

  <xsl:template match="emph">
    <i><xsl:apply-templates/></i>
  </xsl:template>

  <xsl:template match="option">
  </xsl:template>

</xsl:stylesheet>
```

Listing 8.15 Modifications to Enable Formatting of the emph and option Elements

Imported templates are treated differently from included templates. When a matching template is being sought for an element, the ones in the current document are all searched before any of those in an imported document. That means that any templates in the importing document will have precedence over any template in the imported document. Included templates, on the other hand, share the same level of priority as those in the including document; it is their position in the file that determines the priority.

Figure 8.3   Applying Formatting to the Text of Nested Elements

xsl:strip-space and xsl:preserve-space

The xsl:strip-space element can be used to specify a list of one or more element names that will have all the space stripped out of them before any formatting is applied. The syntax is to use the element's attribute to list the element names separated by spaces, as follows:

```
<xsl:strip-space elements="name1 name2 name3 ..."/>
```

The xsl:preserve-space element can be used to specify one or more elements that are to retain spaces and have them formatted along with the other characters in the data. The syntax is the same as xsl:strip-space:

```
<xsl:preserve-space elements="name1 name2 name3 ..."/>
```

Creating a Web Page

When many of the techniques explored earlier in this chapter are used, as they are in Listing 8.15, the XML document in Listing 8.13 can be formatted into the somewhat presentable Web page shown in Figure 8.4.

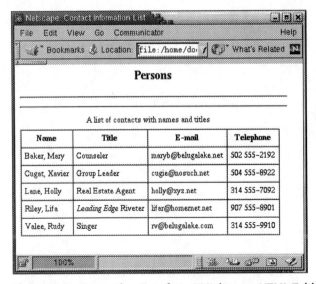

Figure 8.4   Formatting Data from XML into an HTML Table

The table form of the data is created by using the XSL document in Listing 8.16. So long as the same DTD is used (that is, the same tags names are used to mean the same things), the XSL document will be able to dynamically convert the data into the format shown in the figure. The process is entirely automated and can be used as part of a Web site to generate pages as the result of queries coming in from Web browsers. Of course, to use something like this in production, you would want to dress it up a bit more with background colors and perhaps an occasional logo, but the process for doing so is no different from what is already here.

Summary

This chapter began with very simple examples of XSL stylesheet transformations. To use the JAXP to perform a transformation, it is necessary to provide an input XML document to be transformed, an XSL stylesheet to define the transformation, and an output stream or the name of an output file. The entire transformation can then be executed in a single method call. There is complete error checking on both the input document and the stylesheet. If no errors are reported, the result you described in the stylesheet is written to the output.

The next chapter is about the Ant utility, which can be used to manage a Java software development project. It is written in Java, and it knows how to process Java classes and can handle some of the special situations such as packages and classpaths.

```
<?xml version="1.0"?>
<xsl:stylesheet
        xmlns:xsl="http://www.w3.org/1999/XSL/Transform"
        version="1.0">

  <xsl:template match="folks">
    <html>
    <head>
     <title>Contact Information List</title>
    </head>
    <body>
    <center><h1>Persons</h1></center>
    <hr />
    <hr />
    <table border="yes" cellspacing="0" cellpadding="5">
     <caption align="top">
       A list of contacts with names and titles
     </caption>
     <tr>
        <th>Name</th>
        <th>Title</th>
        <th>E-mail</th>
        <th>Telephone</th>
      </tr>
      <xsl:for-each select="person">
        <tr>
          <td><xsl:apply-templates select="name"/></td>
          <td><xsl:apply-templates select="title"/></td>
          <td><xsl:apply-templates select="email"/></td>
          <td><xsl:apply-templates select="phone"/></td>
        </tr>
      </xsl:for-each>
    </table>
    </body>
    </html>
  </xsl:template>

  <xsl:template match="emph">
    <i><xsl:apply-templates/></i>
  </xsl:template>

  <xsl:template match="option">
  </xsl:template>

</xsl:stylesheet>
```

Listing 8.16   XSL Stylesheet to Format a Name List into a Table

CHAPTER

9

Ant

This chapter is about using Ant along with XML control files to compile and execute Java programs. Not only is it useful for managing projects, but Ant is also an example of a large XML application. It uses XML for its control and configuration files and does it by using Java and the JAXP

Ant is a utility program that can facilitate the compiling of Java source code into Java class files, using an XML file as the control file to execute a set of commands. Ant is written in Java in such a way that you can add new commands by simply extending the existing classes and then including these commands in your XML control file to have them execute.

Ant was written to be a replacement for the make utility; it does everything the make utility does and much more. In particular, without modification, Ant understands the things needed to manage a Java development project. If you have ever used make to write a program made from a collection of Java classes, you are familiar with some of the problems in determining which classes need to be compiled and where the packages are located. The main difference between Ant and the make utility is that Ant contains its commands internally as part of its Java code, and the make utility uses shell command lines in its control file (the makefile). You can also use command lines from inside Ant, but most of what you need is already a part of Ant.

The latest version of Ant can be downloaded from its Web site: http://jakarta
.apache.org/ant/. You can download your version of Ant in a binary form ready for installation, or you can download the source code and compile it yourself. The instructions for the installation of Ant come with the download. It is written in Java, and it
uses XML extensively, so you must have the JAXP installed to make it work.

Running Ant from the Command Line

The commands for Ant are stored in an XML file called a *buildfile*. If no other name is
specified on the command line, it is assumed that the buildfile is named `build.xml`,
and Ant looks for it in the current directory. The simplest way to execute Ant is simply
to enter the following command:

```
ant
```

This command will execute instructions in the buildfile named `build.xml`. A buildfile has a number of instructions, called *targets*, that can be executed from the command
line. If you don't specify a target, the default is executed. If you specify a name on the
command line, it is assumed to be the name of a target in the buildfile. For example, the
following command will execute the target named `cleanup` in the buildfile named
`build.xml`:

```
ant cleanup
```

Actually, you can specify more than one target on the command line, and the targets
will each be executed in the order in which you name them. For example, the following command will first execute the target named `cleanup`, then `compile`, and finally
`install`:

```
ant cleanup compile install
```

The general format of the Ant command line is as follows:

```
ant [options] [target [target [target] ... ]]
```

All of the Ant command-line options are listed in Table 9.1.

The Content of the Buildfile

The buildfile file contains a collection of elements, with tag names that are known to
Ant, each of which serves as a specific command or task. Ant reads the buildfile and executes the commands defined inside a target, which can be either the default target or
the target specified on the command line. The commands of the target being executed
may cause the other targets in the file also to be executed.

Table 9.1 The Ant Command-Line Options

OPTION	DESCRIPTION
`-buildfile` *<filename>*	Uses the named file as the buildfile instead of using `build.xml`.
`-D`*<name>*`=`*<value>*	Sets the named property to the specified value. These properties will override any that are set inside the buildfile.
`-debug`	Displays debugging information about the internal processing of Ant itself.
`-emacs`	Displays information in a simplified format suitable for text editing.
`-find` *<filename>*	Searches for the buildfile in the parent directory, and then its parent directory, and so on up the directory tree until either the buildfile is found or the root directory has been searched.
`-help`	Prints a list of the command-line syntax and options.
`-listener` *<classname>*	Adds an instance of the named class as a project listener.
`-log file` *<filename>*	Redirects the output to the named file instead of the display.
`-logger` *<classname>*	The name of the class responsible for logging.
`-projecthelp`	Looks into the buildfile and lists the names of the main targets and subordinate targets.
`-quiet`	Displays less information than usual about Ant processing.
`-verbose`	Displays more information than usual about Ant processing.
`-version`	Displays the Ant version number.

A buildfile contains just one *project*, and a project comprises up to three things:

1. **Targets.** Every project has one or more targets, and one of these is the default target. The default is used when no other target is specified on the command line.

2. **Name.** A project may be assigned a name, although it is not required to have one.

3. **Base directory.** A base directory specifies the location from which all relative path name references are rooted. If it is not specified, the `basedir` property setting is used. If the property is also not specified, the current directory (the one containing the buildfile) is assumed.

Project

The buildfile is an XML file. The root element of the buildfile is a `project` element. Its attributes are the name of the project and the name of the default target. The example buildfile in Listing 9.1 doesn't actually do anything, but it does demonstrate the fundamental syntax of an Ant buildfile and its `project` element. As you can see, Listing 9.1 shows an XML document that has the standard heading, and the `project` element has both an opening and closing tag. In this example, the `target` element has a `name` attribute, and nothing else, and is in the form of an XML opening and closing tag.

The buildfile in Listing 9.1 has a project with the name `"simple"` and the default target is named `"donothing"`. Whenever this buildfile, which is stored in a file with the default name of `build.xml`, is used by Ant, it results in the output shown in Listing 9.2. The buildfile doesn't do anything, but Ant finds no errors, so it considers the result to be a success. The elapsed time of 2 seconds is mostly the startup delay incurred in bringing up a new JVM.

Target

An Ant target is an XML element with the tag name `target`. A target has a `name` attribute and, optionally, the content of the element made up from a set of instructions (called *tasks*) to be executed as the commands of the target. Table 9.2 contains a brief description of the attributes that can be set for a target.

The example shown in Listing 9.3 is a buildfile with a single target that is named `"clean"`. The `project` element declares it as being the default target, so it will exe-

```
<?xml version="1.0"?>

<project name="simple" default="donothing">

<target name="donothing" />

</project>
```

Listing 9.1   A Buildfile with a Name and a Target

```
Buildfile: simple.xml

donothing:

BUILD SUCCESSFUL

Total time: 2 seconds
```

Listing 9.2   Ant Output with No Errors

Table 9.2   The Attributes of the Target Element

NAME	DESCRIPTION
Depends	A comma-separated list of target names that must be executed before this one.
description	A description of the purpose of this target.
if	The name of a property that must be set to allow this target to execute.
name	This is the only required attribute. It is the name of the target.
unless	The name of a property that must not be set to allow this target to execute.

```xml
<?xml version="1.0"?>

<project default="clean">

<target name="clean">
    <delete>
        <fileset dir="." includes="*.class" />
    </delete>
</target>

</project>
```

Listing 9.3   A Project with a Default Target

cute automatically unless some other target is named on the command line of Ant. The "clean" target contains a delete element and inside the delete element is a fileset element that names the set of files to be deleted as all the files in the current directory with the suffix .class. The result is that executing this buildfile will delete all the Java class files from the current directory.

One of the most important capabilities of the buildfile is the ability to have the execution of a target depend on the successful execution of one or more other targets. The tasks inside a target will continue to execute until one of them results in a nonzero value. Any task resulting in a nonzero value will cause the target to immediately cease execution and return a failed status to its caller.

Listing 9.4 shows a project with a default target that depends on the execution of other targets. The default target is named "one" and, because of its depends setting, will only execute after the execution of both "two" and "five". Because the execution of the dependent list is from left to right, the path of execution begins with "two", where it is discovered that that "three", "four", and "five" must all be executed first. An attempt to execute "three" requires that "four" and "five" go first, so "four" is executed. The target named "four" can be executed immediately because it

```
<?xml version="1.0"?>

<project default="one">

<target name="one" depends="two,five">
    <echo message="One"/>
</target>

<target name="two" depends="three,four,five">
    <echo message="Two"/>
</target>

<target name="three" depends="four,five">
    <echo message="Three"/>
</target>

<target name="four">
    <echo message="Four"/>
</target>

<target name="five">
    <echo message="Five"/>
</target>

</project>
```

Listing 9.4   Targets That Depend on Other Targets

has no dependencies. Once "four" executes, backing up one level proceeds as the attempt to execute "three" continues—where it is discovered that "five" must come before it, so "five" is executed. This means that "three" has met its dependency requirements and can be executed immediately. Backing up and continuing to attempt to execute "two", it is discovered that there are other dependencies, but that every one of them has already been satisfied—a target will never be executed more than once. This means that "two" executes immediately and, backing up one level, it is determined that the dependencies of "one" have also been executed, so "one" executes and processing is complete. The output from this process is shown in Listing 9.5.

A target can be instructed to execute conditionally, depending on the presence or absence of a particular property. There are different ways to have properties become set during the execution of a buildfile, as explained later in the "Properties" section. A property is simply a name with a value assigned to it. The following target will execute only if the property named "fromscratch" has been defined with a value:

```
<target name="clean" if="fromscratch">
    <delete>
        <fileset dir="." includes="*.class" />
    </delete>
</target>
```

```
Buildfile: targetdepend.xml

four:
     [echo]  Four

five:
     [echo]  Five

three:
     [echo]  Three

two:
     [echo]  Two

one:
     [echo]  One

BUILD SUCCESSFUL

Total time: 3 seconds
```

Listing 9.5   The Execution Order of Listing 9.4

In similar fashion, the following will only execute if the property named `"saveall"` has *not* been defined:

```
<target name="clean" unless="saveall">
    <delete>
        <fileset dir="." includes="*.class" />
    </delete>
</target>
```

There can be only one `if` and one `unless` attribute defined for a target. If you define both of them in one target, they must both be satisfied for the target to execute. The following is a summary of the rules of target execution:

1. The execution begins with either the default target or the target specified on the command line.

2. No target is executed more than once. After a target has been executed, the dependencies upon it declared for any other targets will all be satisfied.

3. No target will execute until all of the targets it depends on are executed.

4. When a target depends on more than one other target, the other targets are executed in the order in which they are declared (left to right).

5. The presence of an `if` attribute will allow the target to execute only if the named property has been defined. For the purpose of dependencies, the target will be considered to have executed successfully even if the `if` attribute prohibits execution.

6. The presence of an `unless` attribute will allow the target to actually execute only if the named property has not been defined. For the purpose of dependencies, the target will be considered to have executed successfully even if the `unless` attribute prohibits execution.

7. Circular dependencies are detected by Ant and the build will fail with an error message before any targets are executed. That is, if target A depends on B, B depends on C, and C depends on A, Ant will exit with an error message.

Tasks

Inside a `target` element there are normally one or more *task* elements. A task element is an executable command. Many of these tasks are available, and you can even define task elements of your own. (This is what makes it possible for you to customize Ant by extending it to do anything you would like it to do.) To create a new task a Java class must be written that extends one of the existing classes already in Ant.

Probably the simplest of tasks is the one named `echo`, which displays a line of text to the standard output. The following example shows how a couple of tasks can be included in the body of a target:

```
<target name="verbose">
    <echo message="This will display on the console"/>
    <echo message="So will this"/>
</target>
```

Many tasks come with Ant. Each has its own purpose, and each has its own set of attributes that control its actions. Table 9.3 lists all of the standard tasks. Beyond the common ones listed in the table, there are also optional, uncommon ones that come with

Table 9.3   The Built-in Tasks of Ant

NAME	PURPOSE
ant	Execute another buildfile as a subproject
antcall	Execute a target with some property settings that are different from the target being currently executed
antstructure	Generates an Ant buildfile DTD, including all tasks
apply	Executes a command as you would enter it from the command line
available	Sets a property, if a resource is currently available
chmod	Changes the access permissions of one or more files
copy	Copies one or more files
cvs	Handles modules stored in a CVS repository
delete	Deletes one or more files
echo	Outputs text to standard out or to a file

Table 9.3   (*continued*)

NAME	PURPOSE
exec	Executes a command as you would enter it from the command line
execon	Executes a command as you would enter it from the command line
fail	Exits the current `build` with a failure status
filter	Defines filtering to be optionally applied to copied files
fixcrlf	Converts copied text files to the local text format
genkey	Generates a key in the keystore
get	Retrieves a file using a URL
gunzip	Expands a file that was compressed using gzip
gzip	Compresses a set of files into a gzip file
jar	Compresses a set of files into a Java JAR file
java	Executes a Java class
javac	Compiles the Java source tree
javadoc	Generates documentation using the `javadoc` tool
mail	Sends SMTP email
mkdir	Creates a directory
move	Moves a file to a new name and/or directory
patch	Applies a diff file as a patch to text files
property	Sets a property name and value
replace	Substitutes one string for another in a file
rmic	Runs the rmic compiler for a class
signjar	Signs a JAR or zip file using the `javasign` utility
sql	Executes a series of SQL statements
style	Processes a set of documents via XSLT
tar	Stores a set of files in a tar archive file
taskdef	Adds a new task definition
touch	Changes the modification date of a file or directory
tstamp	Generates the current time in hhmm format
unjar	Extracts files compressed by zip or JAR
unwar	Extracts files compressed by zip or JAR
unzip	Extracts files compressed by zip or JAR
uptodate	Sets a property if target files are more up to date than source files
war	A special extension to `jar` to handle WEB-INF files
zip	Compresses a set of files into a zip file

Ant; they do everything from converting native ASCII into Unicode to compiling C# in the .NET environment. Every task has its own set of optional and required attributes. Some of the more useful ones are described later in the "Some Useful Tasks" section, and all of them, both standard and optional, are documented in the HTML documentation that you get with the Ant installation package.

There are detailed descriptions and examples further on in this chapter for using some of the most common tasks listed in Table 9.3. See "Some Useful Tasks."

Properties

An Ant property is a defined name that has been assigned a value string, much the same as a Java property or an environment variable. A property can be defined in different ways and, once a property is defined, the definition can be used in the value of a task attribute or anywhere else you would like textual substitution. By using a property name on the `if` or `unless` attribute of a task, the execution of the task is controlled by whether or not the property has been defined.

There are properties that are predefined and can be used by the tasks in your buildfile. Table 9.4 lists all of these properties by name and explains the meaning of their associated values.

A property can be defined inside a buildfile by using the Ant `property` element as follows:

```
<property name="hostname" value="artast"/>
```

The definition of a property can be placed outside of any of the targets, which will cause it to be defined for all targets before the first target executes. The definition can also be placed inside a target, as if it were one of its tasks, and the property will also become defined for all targets—but only after that particular task has been executed inside the target. In other words, the definition of a property is always global to the entire project once the property task has been executed, but the definition will not occur until a later time if it is done inside a target.

Once a property has been assigned a value, it cannot be changed by executing another property command from inside a target. You can define properties, but you cannot change or undefine them. This limitation may seem a bit restricting at first, but it is very handy for setting a state so that it overrides later attempts to set the same state.

Table 9.4   The Built-in Properties

NAME	VALUE
ant.file	The absolute path of the buildfile.
ant.java.version	The version of the Java Virtual Machine executing Ant. This is the dotted numeric version number such as "1.2" or "1.3".
ant.project.name	The name of the project. This is the value defined on the name attribute of the project element.
basedir	The absolute path of the project's base directory as set by the basedir attribute of the project element.

The same property definition you can make inside the buildfile can also be made from the command line that starts the Ant process, as follows:

```
ant -Dhostname=artast
```

If you define a property on the command line this way, it overrides any definitions that you may attempt to make inside the buildfile. This is because once a property has been set, it cannot be changed.

Environment variables must be included on the command line if they are to be passed to your Ant process. Assuming the environment variable HOSTNAME has been set on your system, that value could be assigned internally by using textual substitution on the command line. For example, on a UNIX system it could be done as follows:

```
ant -Dhostname=$HOSTNAME
```

On a Windows system, it could be done as follows:

```
ant -Dhostname=%HOSTNAME%
```

To extract the value of a property inside a buildfile, all that is necessary is to enclose its name in pair of braces, preceded with a dollar sign, as follows:

```
${hostname}
```

This even works inside a quoted string. The following example will display the name of the host only if the property has been set:

```
<target name="showhost" if="hostname">
    <echo "The host name is ${hostname}"/>
</target>
```

Directory and Filename Pattern Matching

When referring to a file by its name, it is valid to use the wildcard characters * and ?. The * character will match zero or more characters in a file name, and the ? character will match exactly one character in the name. There is also special symbol ** that will match one or more directory levels. Table 9.5 contains some examples of patterns and examples of the files each will match. The table entries show the path names using slash characters, however, it will work the same way on Windows but you must use backslash characters.

There is one bit of shorthand in the pattern. If you end the name of a pattern with a slash or backslash character, a trailing ** is assumed. That is, if you specify big/ the actual pattern used for matching is big/**.

Certain filenames are always automatically excluded. If the name of a file matches any of the exclusion patterns shown in Table 9.6, the filename is ignored even if it matches the pattern you specify. This action can be overridden by setting the following attribute on the element containing a pattern:

```
defaultexcludes="no"
```

Table 9.5   Example Patterns and Filenames That Match and Mismatch

EXAMPLE	MATCHES	DOES NOT MATCH
`*.java`	`fram.java, x.java, J82.java`	`fram.class, x.java.save, java.file`
`?.java`	`x.java, J.java`	`fram.java, x.java.file, J82.java`
`???.java`	`xxx.java, J82.java`	`x.java, xy.java, fram.java, xxx.java.save`
`x/**/*.java`	`x/tm/J82.java, x/frmp/fram.java`	`x/tm/fram.class, x/fram.java`
`**/big/*.java`	`last/big/fram.java, test/max/big/any.java`	`big/fram.java, test/max/any.java`
`big/**`	`big/fram/jum/fram.java, big/x/frmp.class, big/fram.java`	`fram.java, log/big/fram.java`

Table 9.6   Patterns of the Default Exclusions

PATTERN
`**/*~`
`**/#*#`
`**/$*$`
`**/%*%`
`**/CVS`
`**/CVS/**`
`**/.cvsignore`

The default exclusions exist to prevent you from inadvertently including the CVS directory, or any of its contents, and to prevent you from including some special filenames, such as an archive file with a trailing tilde on its name.

Patternset

The `patternset` element is a rule that can be applied to a filename to determine whether it should be included in the set. The rule is generally simple but can get complicated and can be made up of a number of tests. It is even possible to specify a combination of rules that will include or exclude specific files according to patterns in the

Table 9.7 Attributes of the `patternset` Element

ATTRIBUTE	DESCRIPTION
id	An `identification` attribute used to as the buildfile's name of the `patternset`
includes	A comma-separated list of filename patterns for the files to be included
includesfile	The name of a file that contains lines of text, each line being an inclusion pattern
excludes	A comma-separated list of filename patterns for the files to be excluded
excludesfile	The name of a file that contains lines of text, each line being an exclusion pattern

names of the files. Once the rule is defined, and is assigned a unique identification, it can be used anywhere in the buildfile that a list of filenames is required.

There are two ways to specify the patterns that control which filenames are included. You can specify a set of inclusion and exclusion patterns by using the attributes listed in Table 9.7. Alternatively, you can use the two subelements listed in Table 9.8. In either case, an `id` attribute is required to give you a name that you can use to refer to the patternset.

Either of the approaches in Table 9.8 will allow you to specify more than one inclusion and more than one exclusion rule. If you use the attributes, they are in a file or separated by commas. If you use the nested elements, you can repeat each of the two subelements as often as you need to be able to define all the rules.

The following example includes all files in the current directory with a suffix of either `.c` or `.java`:

```
<patternset>
    <include name="*.c,*.java"/>
</patternset>
```

The following example includes all files in the current directory, and those in any subdirectory, that have either the letters axa in their names or end with `.java`, but it will not look in any directory named `test`:

```
<patternset>
    <include name="**/*axa*,**/*.java"/>
    <exclude name="**/test/**"/>
</patternset>
```

Fileset

At times you may want to perform an operation on a group of files. For example, you may want to clean up a directory by deleting all the class files, or you may want to copy only the source files from one directory to another. You can do this by defining a

Table 9.8 Elements Used inside the `patternset` Element

NAME	DESCRIPTION
include	A single pattern that is to be applied to a filename to test for inclusion
exclude	A single pattern that is to be applied to a filename to test for exclusion

Table 9.9 The Attributes for the `fileset` Tag

ATTRIBUTE	DESCRIPTION
dir	The root directory for all files that are members of this set. This is the only required attribute.
defaultexcludes	If the value is set to `"yes"`, the default exclusions will apply; setting it to `"no"` will disable the default exclusions. The default is `"yes"`.
includes	A comma-separated list of patterns that specify the filenames to be included. The default is to include all files.
includesfile	A file that contains lines of text, each line being an inclusion pattern.
excludes	A comma-separated list of filename patterns for the files to be excluded. The default is to exclude no files except the default excludes.
excludesfile	A file that contains lines of text, each line being an exclusion pattern.

`fileset` element that describes the files you want to include in the list. Table 9.9 describes the attributes that are valid for use with the `fileset` tag.

The following example will match all files in the directory named /home/xset that end with .c or .java. It will also match any file in any subdirectory of /home/xset that ends with .java:

```
<fileset dir="/home/xset">
    <patternset>
        <include name="*.c,**/*.java"/>
    </patternset>
</fileset>
```

Path and Classpath

One of the attributes of the `javac` command (the Java compiler) is `classpath`. The value of this attribute is a list of directory and/or JAR filenames. This list of names is separated by colons on some systems and by semicolons on others, but Ant takes care of the separator character for you. All you need to do is specify a path element and list the files and directories separately; when Ant creates the actual path string, it inserts the correct separator character.

The first step in defining a `classpath` is to create a `path` element that lists all of the directories and JAR files, such as the following:

```
<path id="myworkpath">
    <pathelement location="."/>
    <pathelement location="/home/fred/classdir/"/>
    <pathelement location="/usr/local/jaxp/jaxp.jar"/>
    <pathelement location="/usr/local/zproj/zclasses.zip"/>
    <pathelement location="${xproj}/xlimit.jar"/>
</path>
```

You can include as many `pathelement` elements as you need to construct the entire path. Each `pathelement` names a single directory (or JAR file) that contains classes that are needed by the application. This example is for a UNIX system, but the exact same form can be used for a Windows system, which allows the inclusion of colons to specify drive letters and allows the use of backslash characters.

The `path` element has an `id` attribute that is an ID-type attribute that provides the path definition with a unique name. The following example is a `target` element that will compile all of the Java files in the current directory using the previously defined path element with the ID myworkpath as the `classpath`:

```
<target name="compile"/>
    <javac srcdir=".">
        <classpath refid="myworkpath"/>
    </javac>
</target>
```

That's all there is to setting up a basic `path` or `classpath`, but there are some other things you can do. For example, to extend the previously defined `path`, you can include it in a new `path` definition, as follows:

```
<path id="myextendedpath">
    <path refid="myworkpath"/>
    <pathelement location="/home/sam/classes"/>
</path>
```

You can insert a `fileset` element as in the following example, which will include all of the JAR files in a specific directory tree:

```
<path id="treepath">
    <fileset dir="/home/fred/lib">
        <include name="**/*.jar"/>
    </fileset>
    <pathelement location="/home/sam/classes"/>
</path>
```

Some Useful Tasks

All of the built-in tasks of Ant are listed in Table 9.3, and most of them have both optional and required attributes. Some of them have nested elements that can be used in addition to, or in place of, the attributes. This section describes the attributes and nested elements of some the tasks that are most commonly used to set up a Java development project.

`available`

This task will set the value of a property depending on whether some resource is currently available. The resource in question can be a class found somewhere along the `classpath`, a resource accessible through the JVM, or a file. The attributes are listed in Table 9.10 and the nested element is listed in Table 9.11. The minimum requirements are the name of the property and the specifications of the resource.

The following will set the property named `havemuck` to `"true"` if the file named `muck.java` exists:

```
<available file="/home/fred/muck.java" property="havemuck"/>
```

Table 9.10   Attributes of the `available` Task

NAME	DESCRIPTION
classname	A property. The name of a class somewhere on the `classpath`. Required if neither `resource` nor `file` is specified.
classpath	A `classpath` string. If the `classname` resource is specified, only this `classpath` will be used, if it is specified.
classpathref	The reference to an ID name of a `classpath` element. If the `classname` resource is specified, only this `classpath` will be used if it is specified.
file	A property. The name of a single file. Required if neither `classname` nor `resource` is specified.
property	The name of the property to be set. Required.
resource	A property. A resource of the JVM. Required if neither `classname` nor `file` is specified.
value	The value string to be assigned to the property. The default is `"true"`.

Table 9.11   Nested Element of the `available` Task

NAME	DESCRIPTION
classpath	Instead of using either of the `classpath` attribute settings, this element can be used to specify the path.

The following will set the property named `"transtat"` to the value `"havexform"` if the class `Transform` is present somewhere on the path specified by the path with the ID name `"myworkpath"`:

```
<available class="javax.xml.transform.Transform" property="transtat"
        classpathref="myworkpath" value="havexform"/>
```

chmod

The `chmod` task will change the permissions settings for one or more files and/or directories. In the current version of Ant this only works on UNIX systems, and the permission settings are the UNIX-style names and values. The attributes for `chmod` are listed in Table 9.12 and the nested element is listed in Table 9.13.

Table 9.12   Attributes of the `chmod` Task

NAME	DESCRIPTION
dir	The name of a single directory containing the files to have their permissions changed. Required if neither the `id` attribute nor the nested `fileset` element is specified.
defaultexcludes	If set to `"yes"`, the default exclusions apply; if set to `"no"`, they don't apply. The default is `"yes"`.
excludes	A comma-separated list of file patterns to be excluded. If this is not specified, the default exclusions are applied.
excludesfile	The name of a text file that contains one file pattern per line. Each line is assumed to be an `exclude` pattern.
file	The name of a single file or directory that is to have its permissions changed. Required if neither the `id` attribute nor the nested `fileset` element is specified.
includes	A comma-separated list of file patterns to be included. If this is not specified, all files are included.
includesfile	The name of a text file containing one file pattern per line. Each line is assumed to be an `include` pattern.
parallel	If set to `"true"`, all files are processed using a single UNIX `chmod` command. If set to `"false"`, a separate command is used for each file. The default is `"true"`.
perm	The new permissions in any of the forms that are known to the UNIX `chmod` command-line utility. Required.
type	If set to `"file"`, permissions will only be changed for files. If set to `"dir"`, permissions will only be changed for directories. If set to `"both"`, permissions will be altered for both directories and files. The default is `"file"`.

Table 9.13   Nested Element of the `chmod` Task

NAME	DESCRIPTION
fileset	Can be used to specify the names of the files and/or directories to have their permissions altered.

The following modifies the permissions of the file named `/home/bin/setup.sh` so that it is can be read and executed by anyone

```
<chmod file="/home/bin/setup.sh" perm="ugo+rx"/>
```

The following sets the permissions on every file beneath the directory named `/home/bin` that is also beneath a directory named `test`, and every file addressed by the `fileset` with the ID `"workfiles"`, have their permissions set to the pattern defined by `0755`:

```
<chmod perm="0755">
    <fileset dir="/home/bin">
        <include name="**/test/**"/>
    </fileset>
    <fileset refid="workfiles"/>
</chmod>
```

copy

The `copy` task duplicates a file, a collection of files, or a collection of files and directories. A mapper can be used to change the names of the files as they are copied. It is also possible to specify whether destination files are to be overwritten. The attributes are listed in Table 9.14, and the nested elements are listed in Table 9.15.

The following copies the file named `build.xml` to the file named `backup.xml`:

```
<copy file="build.xml" tofile="backup.xml"/>
```

The following copies the file named `build.xml` into the directory named `backup`:

```
<copy file="build.xml" todir="../backup"/>
```

The following copies an entire directory named `devel`, along with all its contents, into a directory named `util/backup`:

```
<copy todir="../util/backup"/>
    <fileset dir="devel"/>
</copy>
```

The following copies an entire directory named `devel`, along with all its contents, into a directory named `util/backup` and changes the name of all files with the suffix `.java` into files with the suffix `.back`:

Table 9.14 Attributes of the `copy` Task

NAME	DESCRIPTION
`file`	The name of a file to be copied. This is required unless a nested `fileset` element is used.
`preservelastmodified`	If set to `"yes"`, the modification date is copied from the original file. If set to `"no"`, the modification date is set to the current time. The default is `"no"`.
`filtering`	If set to `"yes"`, token filtering will take place in the copied files. The default is `"no"`.
`includeEmptyDirs`	If set to `"yes"`, empty directories at the source are copied to the destination. If set to `"no"`, empty directories are ignored. The default is `"yes"`.
`overwrite`	If set to `"yes"`, any destination files that already exist will be overwritten. The default is `"no"`.
`flatten`	If set to `"yes"`, the source directory structure is ignored and all files are copied into the single destination directory specified by `todir`. The default is `"no"`.
`todir`	The name of the destination directory of the copy. This can be used with the `file` attribute or with a nested `fileset`.
`tofile`	The name of the destination file of the copy. This can only be used along with the `file` attribute.

Table 9.15 Nested Elements of the `copy` Task

NAME	DESCRIPTION
`fileset`	Can be used to specify the names of the files and/or directories to be copied.
`mapper`	Can be used to map source filenames to destination filenames.

```
<copy todir="../util/backup"/>
    <fileset dir="devel"/>
    <mapper type="glob" from="*.java" to="*.back"/>
</copy>
```

delete

The `delete` task deletes one or more files and/or directories. The attributes are listed in Table 9.16, and the nested element is listed in Table 9.17.

The following example deletes the single file named `rimp.class`:

```
<delete file="/home/lib/rimp.class"/>
```

Table 9.16 Attributes of the `delete` Task

NAME	DESCRIPTION
`dir`	The name of the directory containing files to be deleted. This is required unless the `file` attribute is specified or a nested `fileset` element is used.
`file`	The name of a file to be copied. This is required unless the `dir` attribute is specified or a nested `fileset` element is used.
`quiet`	If set to `"true"`, there is no error reported if the file or directory to be deleted does not exist. If set to `"false"`, an error is reported and the exit status of the task is set to a failed condition. The default is `"false"`.
`includeEmptyDirs`	If set to `"true"`, empty directories will be deleted when they are specified in a `fileset`. If set to `"false"`, empty directories are not deleted. The default is `"false"`.
`verbose`	If set to `"true"`, the name of each file and directory is displayed as it is deleted. The default is `"false"`.

Table 9.17 Nested Element of the `delete` Task

NAME	DESCRIPTION
`fileset`	Can be used to specify the names of the files and/or directories to be deleted.

The following deletes the directory named /home/lib, along with all its contents, and will not report an error if the directory does not exist:

```
<delete dir="/home/lib" quiet="true"/>
```

The following deletes all files that are in the directory named ../safety or any of its subdirectores. The directory named ../safety is not deleted, but all subdirectories, empty or not, will be deleted:

```
<delete includeEmptyDirs="true">
    <fileset dir="../safety"/>
</delete>
```

echo

The echo task will output text to either the standard output or to a file. The attributes of the echo task are listed in Table 9.18.

The following displays a line of text:

```
<echo message="This text will display"/>
```

Table 9.18 Attributes of the `echo` Task

NAME	DESCRIPTION
message	The character text to be output. Required unless the `echo` element contains nested text.
file	The name of the file to receive the output text. If it not specified, the text goes to the standard output.
append	If set to `"true"`, and the `file` attribute is specified, the output text will be appended to the end of the file. If `"false"`, the output text will overwrite the file. The default is `"false"`.

The following will display more than one line of text:

```
<echo>
It is possible to have a single echo command write
more than one line of text by including the body
of the text inside the element.
</echo>
```

exec

The `exec` task can be used to execute a system command just as if it had been entered from the command prompt. Your Ant processing will halt and wait for the command to complete. The attributes are listed in Table 9.19, and the nested elements are listed in Table 9.20.

The available nested elements are `arg` and `env`, and their attributes are listed in Tables 9.21 and 9.22. The `arg` element is used to specify a list of one or more arguments to be included on the command line. The `env` element will set environment variables for the execution of the command.

The following example will execute a command called `dir` and store the output in a file named `dirlist.txt`:

```
<exec executable="dir" output="dirlist.txt"/>
```

The following will execute only on the Linux operating system. The program executed is a2ps, and it will operate on the file named `descrip.txt` in the current directory. It will run a2ps with the `--glob` option.

```
<exec executable="a2ps" os="Linux">
    <arg line="--glob descrip.txt"/>
</exec>
```

The following example executes a command named `pathfind` with the argument string `"-J -m vetline"`. The PATH environment variable is set to the one defined by

Table 9.19 Attributes of the `exec` Task

NAME	DESCRIPTION
`dir`	The directory in which the command is to be executed.
`executable`	The command to be executed. It must be specified here without its command-line arguments. Required.
`newenvironment`	If set to `"true"`, the existing environment variables are not propagated to the environment of the command being executed. The default is `"false"`.
`failonerror`	If set to `"true"`, the return code from the command is any value other than zero, and the build process will halt with an error. The default is `"false"`.
`os`	The name of the operating system. If this is specified, the command will execute only if the current operating system is the one named. The default is to execute the command for any operating system.
`output`	The file to which any output is to be directed. The default is for the output to go to standard output.
`timeout`	Kill the command if it does not complete within the specified duration. The duration is in milliseconds. The default is to allow the command to execute forever.

Table 9.20 Nested Elements of the `exec` Task

NAME	DESCRIPTION
`arg`	Specifies the list of arguments appended to the command line.
`env`	Specifies new environment variables that are to be set in the environment of the command being executed.

Table 9.21 Attributes of the `arg` Element of the `exec` Task

NAME	DESCRIPTION
`file`	The name of a file that contains a single line of text that is to be used as the argument passed to the command. Required if no other attribute is specified.
`line`	Specifies any number of space-separated command-line arguments. Required if no other attribute is specified.
`path`	A string that will be treated as a path. It may be specified using either colon or semicolon separators. Required if no other attribute is specified.
`value`	Specifies a single command-line argument (which may contain spaces). Required if no other attribute is specified.

Table 9.22 Attributes of the `env` Element of the `exec` Task

NAME	DESCRIPTION
file	The absolute path name of the named file will be used as the value of the environment variable. Required if neither `path` nor `value` is present.
key	The name of the environment variable. Required.
path	A string that will be treated as a path and assigned to the environment variable. It may be specified using either colon or semicolon separators. Required if neither `value` nor `file` is present.
value	The value to be assigned to the environment variable. Required if neither `path` nor `file` is present.

the property named `workpath`. The command will be allowed to execute for no more than 2 seconds.

```
<exec executable="pathfind" timeout="2000">
    <env key="PATH" path="${workpath}"/>
    <arg line="-J -m vetline"/>
</exec>
```

java

The `java` task will execute a Java class in the JVM running Ant, or it can be instructed to start a new JVM to run class. If you decide to execute a class in the current JVM, the class should not call `System.exit()` because that will halt the JVM, which will also halt Ant.

The only required attribute is the name of the class to be executed. The list of available attributes is shown in Table 9.23, and the available nested elements are listed in Table 9.24.

The following example executes a class named `LoadTree` found in the file named `LoadTree.class` in the current directory:

```
<java classname="LoadTree"/>
```

The following will execute a class named `LoadTree` in a separate JVM. The JVM will search for classes on the path defined by the `classpath` definition with the ID name `"myclasspath"`. The argument passed to the class is the filename `plist.xml` in the directory named `sources`.

```
<java classname="LoadTree" fork="yes">
    arg value="../sources/plist.xml"/>
    <classpath refid="myclasspath"/>
</java>
```

Table 9.23   Attributes of the `java` Task

NAME	DESCRIPTION
`classname`	The name of the class to be executed. Required.
`classpath`	The `classpath` to be used for the execution.
`classpathref`	The ID name of a `classpath` element used to define the `classpath`.
`dir`	The name of the directory in which the new JVM is to be executed, if `fork` is set to `"yes"`.
`failonerror`	If set to `"yes"`, and `fork` is set to `"yes"`, the build process will start if the error code returned from the execution is any value other than 0. The default is `"no"`.
`fork`	If set to `"yes"`, the class will be executed in a separate JVM. The default is `"no"`.
`jvm`	The command used to invoke the new JVM if `fork` is set to `"yes"`. The default is `"java"`.
`maxmemory`	The maximum amount of memory to be allocated to the new JVM, if `fork` is set to `"yes"`.
`output`	The name of a file that will receive the standard output of the executed class.

Table 9.24   Nested Elements of the `java` Task

NAME	DESCRIPTION
`arg`	The arguments to be passed to the class being executed. The attributes are the same as those for `arg` listed in Table 9.21.
`jvmarg`	The arguments to be passed to the new JVM that is executing the class. The attributes are the same as those for `arg` listed in Table 9.21.
`sysproperty`	Defines variables that will be set in the environment of the class being executed. The attributes are the same as those listed for `env` in Table 9.22.
`classpath`	A `classpath` element can be used instead of using a `classpath` attribute.

javac

The `javac` task will compile one or more Java source files into Java class files. Only a Java source file with no class file, or with a class file that is older than the source file, will be compiled.

The only required attribute is the one named `srcdir`, and it is required only in the absence of a nested element named `src`. One of these two must be used to specify the location of the input source file or files. All of the available attributes are listed in Table 9.25, and the available nested elements are in Table 9.26.

Table 9.25 Attributes of the `javac` Task

NAME	DESCRIPTION
bootclasspath	This `classpath` is used to locate the bootstrap classes.
classpath	This `classpath` is to used to locate the class files required by the classes being compiled.
destdir	The name of the root of the directory tree containing the output class file or files. The default is to use the source directory.
debug	If `"on"`, the output class files contain debug information. The default is `"off"`.
depend	If set to `"true"` and the compiler has the capability of checking dependencies, the capability is enabled. The default is `"false"`.
deprecation	If `"on"`, the output class files are compiled with deprecation information. The default is `"off"`.
encoding	The encoding algorithm used on the source files.
excludes	A comma-separated list of filename patterns for the files to be excluded.
excludesfile	A file that contains lines of text, each line being an exclusion pattern.
defaultexcludes	If set to `"no"`, the default file exclusions are not imposed. The default is `"yes"`.
extdirs	This path is used to locate any installed extensions.
failonerror	If `"true"`, the entire build will fail if there is a compilation error. If `"false"`, the build will continue to conclusion, even in the presence of errors. The default is `"true"`.
includeAntRuntime	If set to `"yes"`, the Ant runtime is included. The default is `"yes"`.
includes	A comma-separated list of filename patterns for the files to be included.
includesfile	A file that contains lines of text, each line being an inclusion pattern.
optimize	If `"on"`, the output class files are optimized. The default is `"off"`.
srcdir	The name of the root of the directory tree that contains the source file or files. Required unless the nested element `src` is used.
target	The name of a specific Java version of the output class files. The version numbers are in the form `"1.2"` and `"1.3"`. The default is the version of the compiling program.
verbose	If `"true"`, there is verbose output from the compiler operation. The default is `"false"`.

Table 9.26 Nested Elements of the `javac` Task

NAME	DESCRIPTION
src	A `path` element that can be used in place of the `src` attribute.
classpath	A `path` element that can be used in place of the `classpath` attribute.
bootclasspath	A `path` element that can be used in place of the `bootclasspath` attribute.
extdirs	A `path` element that can be used in place of the `extdirs` attribute.

The following example compiles the source files in the directory tree rooted at the current directory, placing the resulting class files in the same directories, using the `classpath` with the ID name `"myclasspath"`:

```
<javac srcdir=".">
    <classpath refid="myclasspath"/>
</javac>
```

The following compiles all Java source files under the directory named in the property `srcdir` and uses the class files in `working.jar` as the `classpath` to locate needed class files:

```
<javac srcdir="${srcdir}" classpath="working.jar"/>
```

mkdir

The `mkdir` task will create a new directory. If the name of the new directory includes a path name, any nonexistent directories along the path are also created. The only attribute available is `dir`, which specifies the name of the directory. The following example creates a directory, within the current directory, named `workfiles`:

```
<mkdir dir="workfiles"/>
```

The following example creates a path of directories named `dist/config/loading` beneath the directory specified by the `devel` property:

```
<mkdir dir="${devel}/dist/config/loading"/>
```

move

The `move` task will move one or more files or directories from one location to another. This task is similar to the `copy` task, except when files are moved, they no longer exist in their original location.

For the method of selecting files to be moved, refer to the `copy` task. The attributes for `move` are listed in Table 9.27.

Table 9.27 Attributes of the move Task

NAME	DESCRIPTION
file	The name of a file to be moved. This is required unless a nested fileset element is used.
filtering	If set to "yes", token filtering will take place in the copied files. The default is "no".
flatten	If set to "yes", the source directory structure is ignored and all files are copied into the single destination directory specified by todir. The default is "no".
includeEmptyDirs	If set to "yes", empty directories at the source are copied to the destination. If set to "no", empty directories are ignored. The default is "yes".
overwrite	If set to "yes", any destination files that already exist will be overwritten. If set to "no", the destination file is left intact and the source file retains its original position. The default is "yes".
tofile	The name of the destination file to be moved. This can only be used along with the file attribute.
todir	The name of the destination directory of the move. This can be used with either the file attribute or with a nested fileset.

Summary

This chapter described the workings of the Ant utility as an XML application that you can use as a tool when developing software. Not only is it capable of managing Java projects, it also contains the capability of managing projects in several other languages. The process is controlled by an XML file in which the Ant commands are specified by XML elements and attributes. Ant is written in Java so that it can be made to run almost anywhere, and it can be extended by adding classes to process new commands.

The next chapter looks at some things that may be coming up in the future of XML. Although it is always a bit tricky to try to predict the future, some of the items discussed are already well into development and testing.

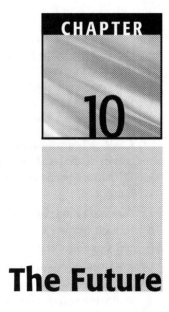

CHAPTER

10

The Future

With the rapid increase in popularity of XML, it is very difficult to determine exactly what is going to happen in the future. New uses for XML are constantly being discovered. The basic idea of being able to store data in a standard format in a way that it can be easily extracted and processed is very attractive. There are many projects underway that are designed to do something special with XML, such as the development of multilingual text processing and a standard XML database. It is not possible to say which of these will succeed or which will even become useful, but the expanding world of XML is making lots of room for experimentation.

This chapter is not an attempt to predict the future. Instead, it describes project ideas currently under consideration or development. Some will succeed, some will fail, and some may not be completed, but it looks like XML is going to be doing a lot more than the original designers imagined.

JAXB

The Java Architecture for XML Binding (JAXB) project at Sun Microsystems is developing a set of utilities that could possibly become an optional package that works with Java 2. Those utilities can be used to convert XML schemas into Java classes. The resulting classes can be used to parse any XML document, based on the same schema as the generated class, and produce a formatted output document.

The generated classes contain code that checks that an incoming document is well-formed and validates it against the DTD used to generate the class. It does its parsing very much like a DOM parser. That is, it produces a memory-resident tree, but it uses only the DTD that was the basis for generating the classes. There is no facility to allow an application to manipulate the parse tree, but there is an API that enables an application to access the tree.

The following are the steps required to create JAXB classes:

1. **Create a binding schema.** You can do this by accepting the binding schema generated by the JAXB or, if you prefer, you can write your own schema based on the DTD that specifies the documents. The schema is written using the JAXB Binding Language.

2. **Generate the Java source files.** Use the JAXB schema compiler, with the schema written in the JAXB Binding Language as input, to generate output that is the source code of the Java classes.

3. **Compile the generated Java classes**. These compiled classes will contain code that will parse an incoming XML document into a tree, validate the resulting tree against the schema, and output the parse tree into a new document.

4. **Write an application.** Use the API found in the generated classes to write an application to perform an XML transformation.

The early version of the JAXB Binding Language is simply a subset of the existing XML DTD language. Because of the limitations inherent in DTD, however, future versions will almost certainly have special extensions or modifications to provide the information necessary to describe all the possibilities of the generated code. A limited number of options are available to automatically generate the binding schema, but this number is almost certain to expand. The ideal situation would be for the automatically produced schema to be complete, but this would require descriptive information to be added to the code. Perhaps DTD itself will be expanded or a more flexible schema language will become widely used. It would be a great advantage to be able to always generate the binding schema from the DTD because there is a tracking problem in keeping the two versions in sync with each other—every time the DTD is changed, the manually created schema also have to be changed.

JAXM

The Java API for XML Messaging (JAXM) project at Sun Microsystems is developing an API to enable applications to send and receive XML-formatted documents using a pure Java API. JAXM is initially intended to be an optional package available for Java 2, but, depending on its success and its level of facility, it may become a standard part of the Java 2 Enterprise Edition.

JAXM is intended to provide a foundation set of APIs that can be used as the basis of higher-level message protocols. It is being implemented as a lightweight API that will enable the development of XML-based messaging systems. An application can be used in the data transmission for something as public as a Web service or as private as a protocol for interoffice data transmission. Conceptually, all communications are between a client (the receiver of a message) and a provider (the sender of a message), but both ends of the link can act as a client or provider.

Internally, the JAXM API is being based on the emerging standard, Simple Object Access Protocol (SOAP), which transmits and receives attachments using the Hypertext Transfer Protocol (HTTP). SOAP is a simple set of conventions that can be used to transmit data without any modifications to the existing HTTP protocol.

JAXR

The Java API for XML Registries (JAXR) project at Sun Microsystems is an API that provides standard access methods that can be used to communicate with registries to build, deploy, and locate Web services. It is intended to be a single API that can be used as an abstraction for any number of existing APIs that are currently used for access to various registries. Several, somewhat overlapping, registry definitions exist, such as OASIS, eCo Framework, ISO 11179, ebXML, and UDDI. Each of these registry systems has its own API, and JAXR is intended to be an umbrella API to make them all look the same to your application.

JAXR is also intended to provide interoperability to a set of open registries that otherwise cannot exchange information. The information from one registry can be stored as a Java object and shared with other registries. Currently, extending the capabilities of all registries by providing a clean path of communication among them is being planned. The same API can be used to extract information from one and store it into another.

The current JAXR development is for an optional package for use with Java 2, but it could possibly be added as part of a future version of the Java 2 Enterprise Edition.

JAX-RPC

The Java API for XML-Based Remote Procedure Calls (JAX-RPC) project at Sun Microsystems is an API to provide a transport-independent set of XML-based remote procedure call protocols. A method running in one computer will have the ability, by transmitting a method name and calling sequence to another computer, to execute a method inside a program running on another computer. The caller of the remote method will be able to pass arguments to the remote procedure and retrieve results from it.

The API is being based on the developing standard of the XML-based remote procedure calling protocol being developed by the W3C Protocol Working Group. The goal of this JAX-RPC project is to develop a set of Java APIs that can be used as an interface to XML protocol. Along with methods to register callable remote methods and to transmit messages, the API will include methods for marshalling and unmarshalling (packing and unpacking) data for transmission and retrieval.

There are two existing RPC systems that are directly accessible from Java—the OMG CORBA Object Request Broker and the standard Java Remote Method Invocation (RMI)—but neither one of these is based on XML.

Initially, the JAX-RPC will be an optional API for the Java 2 Standard Edition, but it is expected to be included as part of a future version of either the Java 2 Standard Edition or the Java 2 Enterprise Edition.

Long-Term JavaBeans Persistence

Java persistence has existed, in the form of serialized objects, since the first version of Java. The persistence technique, known as *serialization*, has always been used to convert the entire contents of a Java object to a stream of ASCII characters. These characters contain not only the class definition of the object but also all of the data that defines the current state of the object. When this information is used, the object can be loaded and started again exactly where it left off. That is, the state of the object persists.

XML is an ideal format for a serialized object, and there is a project that has specified and implemented the use of XML for long-term persistence of objects. One of the main purposes of using XML is to create a form of serialized objects that will persist from one version of Java to another. The existing API for persistence was devised to be as portable as possible but, if you have ever done work with it, you may be aware of the problems that occur when you move from one version of Java to the next. The newer technology of XML is a superior way of doing the same thing because versions will not require a change in the data format.

The previously existing framework of transmitting, storing, and retrieving serialized objects remains the same, but the form of serialized objects is an XML document. This technique is a part of version 1.4 of Java 2 Standard Edition.

Linking

Many more things can be done with Internet linking than with HTML linking. For example, with HTML the link is only in one direction, and it must be hard-coded in the HTML document. This restriction both is inconvenient and, over time, as the Internet changes, results in documents with links that no longer point to anything. With XML, and the ability of XML to use tags to define things about the data it contains, links can be made according to content instead of simply by a location on the Internet. This cannot be done with HTML because the elements all deal with formatting, not with context.

For example, a lot of research has been done on possible linking techniques and things that can be done with linking to create dynamic hypertext documents, which has produced positive results. A link can be defined by the context of the data instead of by a hard-coded URL. Links can be defined as bidirectional, making it possible to surf the Web both forward and backward. This capability leads to the ability to have a single link address multiple locations, all of which are dynamically defined to prevent links to pages that no longer exit. With XML, links can be defined in rings, making it possible to enter the circle of pages at any point and sequentially move through them all and finally return to the page on which you started. The links can be connected in such a way that multiple documents in different locations appear in the browser as a single document without regard to which of the locations was originally addressed.

There is more than one way to achieve dynamic and flexible linking. For example, it would be possible to define link types by using attributes on the element to specify how the link is to be achieved. There could be new types in the DTD used to define the data name and how it is to be linked and specifying the element name used for locating the data in a remote document.

Stylesheets

The formatting rules defined in stylesheets, as they exist now, are somewhat limited. A stylesheet could possibly provide several optional ways of formatting each data element, and then a Web browser (or the software creating a Web page) could be made capable of selecting the form of display according to size, speed, or some other criteria. All of this could operate based on a standard syntax that would make the same data accessible to all kinds of display facilities, from full-screen Web browsers to hand-held devices. For example, a device could make a request to have the data sent to it as large, compact, tiny, or some other form. The device knows the type of data it is capable of displaying and would request that the data be formatted that way. Another approach would be to let the stylesheet specify minimum and maximum dimensions that the viewer could use as a guide to specify its most convenient size.

Stylesheets could include relational information that makes it easy for the user of a Web browser to view the organization of the data and then use this organization to explore the details of the data. The stylesheet could allow the use of special selectors that would select the language to be used to display the data; this would include specifying formatting for left-to-right and right-to-left text. Perhaps partial renderings could be defined, allowing the viewer to select small panels and then flip from one to the other or scroll them through a smaller window. Numeric data could be presented in dynamically dimensioned tables and graphs, which would allow the device to specify the dimensions and have the data formatted to fit it.

The variety of ways to display data is unlimited, and all of these could be expressed in a suitably flexible stylesheet language.

Other Things Are Coming

Almost everywhere you look there are new XML projects getting started. Some projects are so new that they only have names and consist only of a few vague ideas. Others don't even have a firm name yet.

Imagine an IDE that reads the DTD (or schema) and pops up a window full of drag-and-drop objects that you can use to lay out the display. The software inspects the definitions found in the DTD, makes decisions about the sort of things it finds, and provides the user with a set of options that can be applied to the display of each element. Once the individual elements have their displays configured, they can then be used in some sort of drag-and-drop capability to lay out the display. The output from this program could be XSL that would process the data into the display, or it could be a program that reads an incoming XML document, processes it with the user-defined display definitions, and produces appropriate HTML. Alternatively, the program could produce Portable Data Format (PDF) to display the text or just output a JPEG or PNG image.

An XML database could be created. The same DTD (or schema) used to define the data layout could be used to define the layout of the data records in the data files. XML could be used to define the data layouts quite well. All that is needed is some way to organize and store the data in such a way that key values can be used for retrieval. That is, the database software would have all the capabilities of keyed or relational file systems, with the input and output data being in XML format. The same effect could be produced by using an XML/data front end on an existing database system. Suddenly the data itself becomes so portable that it can be transported from one database to another without modification.

These are just some of the reasons why you hear people say, "XML is the future." It just makes things so convenient.

Summary

There are a number of advantages to XML. The ones explored in this book include the fact that the raw XML data can be read by a human, the data can also be read easily by a computer program, it is a simple process to test the format of the data to make certain it is valid, and all or part of the data can be modified without any effect on the rest of data stored in the same document. There are literally hundreds of software utilities that can be used to manipulate an XML document and the data it contains. And there has never before been a format for storing data that allows both the general layout and the data itself to be modified so easily. You will never be locked into a record layout with XML, so there is no problem in designing your data storage to be optimized. This means that you can just come up with a design, start using it today, and change it whenever you decide you have found a better way.

Maybe XML is the future. I certainly plan to use it a lot. Everything you need is on the Internet and free for the taking.

Glossary

attribute   A named parameter value added to an element to modify or amplify the definition of the element.

callback   A method or function that is to be called on the occurrence of some event.

document   Any XML-formatted data is referred to as a document. This means, in XML, that the term *document* has the definition of being any stream of data encapsulated in, and defined by, a set of markup tags.

DOM (Document Object Model)   A parser that isolates the tokens of the input document and stores them in the form of a RAM-resident tree that maintains the relationships of the input document.

DTD (Document Type Definition)   The portion of an XML document used to specify the names and the syntax of the element tags.

element   A single unit of data inside an XML document. It is delimited on the front by an opening tag and on the back by a closing tag, and it may contain other elements.

empty element   An element that has no content between its opening and closing tags.

entity   A name that, when used in text preceded by an & character and terminated by a ; character, expands to the characters defined for that name.

HTML (Hypertext Markup Language)   A simple markup language used to create hypertext documents for the World Wide Web.

HTTP (Hypertext Transfer Protocol)   A TCP/IP protocol used by the World Wide Web to transfer documents from one location to another.

IANA (Internet Assigned Numbers Authority)   The central registry for Internet-assigned numbers, such as protocol ID numbers and well-known port numbers.

ISO (International Organization of Standards)   A voluntary organization founded in 1946 as a repository for international standards, including computer and communications standards.

Java Virtual Machine *See* JVM.

JAXB (Java Architecture for XML Binding)   A set of utilities that convert XML schemas into Java classes that handle the details of parsing and formatting XML documents.

JAXM (Java API for XML Messaging)   An API that enables programs to send and receive XML-formatted documents.

JAXP (Java API for XML Processing)   An API that contains Java parsers and XSL transformation utilities.

JAXR (Java API for XML Registries)   An API that provides standard access methods to registries for building, deploying, and locating Web services.

JAX-RPC (Java API for XML-based RPC)   An API that provides a transport-independent set of XML-based remote procedure call protocols.

JVM (Java Virtual Machine)   The software that interprets and executes Java code.

lexical scanner   A program that reads an input text stream and organizes the characters into tokens (words, numbers, punctuation, etc).

namespace   A naming convention used to organize tag names into groups. The same name can be used in two different groups (namespaces) without conflict.

nested element   An element that is defined in the DTD as being inserted into the body of another element.

parser   A program that reads the token stream input from a text file and organizes the tokens according to a set of syntax rules. *Also see* lexical scanner.

parse tree   The DOM parser loads an XML document into a memory-resident tree and returns the root node of the tree to the application. All the nodes are connected together in a way that can be accessed by the application.

PI (Processing Instruction)   A PI can be included in an XML document to pass special instruction to the process that reads the document. A PI begins with the characters <? and ends with ?>. The heading on each XML document is a special case of a PI.

root   The outermost element (tag pair) of an XML document. It is the element that contains all the other elements and data of the document.

SAX (Simple API for XML)   A parser that tokenizes an input XML document and passes the tokens to a process in the same order in which they appear in the original document.

schema   A document that specifies location and types of data stored in a record. There are schemas for databases, and there are applications that use a schema in place of an XML DTD.

SGML (Standard Generalized Markup Language)   A generic markup language from which XML, HTML, and XHTML are all derived.

SOAP (Simple Object Access Protocol)   A relatively simple set of conventions for executing instructions over HTTP.

standard in, standard out   The default input and output stream of a program.

stylesheet   A document that specifies the transformations that are to be applied to change the format of a document.

tag   A name, and possibly some attributes, surrounded by < and > characters, used as the opening and closing markers for an element inside an XML document.

token   The smallest logical piece in a stream of input text being parsed. A token is a word, punctuation, number, quoted string, or so on.

transform   The process of reading the contents of an XML document, possibly making changes to its content, and writing it back to the original (or possibly a different) form.

tree   *See* parse tree.

URI (Universal Resource Identifier) For practical purposes, this is the same as a URL. Strings of this kind are used by XML to guarantee uniqueness.

URL (Uniform Resource Locator) The partial or full name that uniquely addresses a single resource or file on the World Wide Web, which could be on the local host. A URL is a URI.

valid An XML document is said to be valid only if all of its tags conform to the specifications of a DTD.

well-formed An XML document is said to be well-formed if all of its elements have proper opening and closing tags, the tags are nested properly, and the attribute names and values are properly formatted.

XHTML An HTML document that is also a well-formed XML document. All tags are standard HTML 4 tag names. All elements have both opening and closing tags, and all tags are matched and nested properly.

XML (Extensible Markup Language) A subset of SGML used to mark up documents that contain either data records or text.

XPath A pattern-matching language used inside XSL to select nodes in the incoming parse tree.

XSL (Extensible Style Language) A stylesheet language that can be used to specify the conversion process for converting an XML document to another form.

XSLT (XSL Transformation) The vocabulary of commands that specify the conversions in XSL.

Index